There may not be that much to see in Mount Airy, but what you hear makes up for the difference

LHP

Written or Edited by Thomas D. Perry

Beyond Mayberry

A Memoir of Andy Griffith and Mount Airy North Carolina
By Thomas D. Perry

**The 2020 60th Anniversary of
The Andy Griffith Show
REVISED EDITION**

Reed Perry, Grant Perry, and the author's mother Betty Hobbs Perry at the statue of Andy and Opie going fishing in Mount Airy, North Carolina.

For my mother, Betty Jane Hobbs Perry

For you, "Constant Reader," as Stephen King might say, have an enjoyable read about Andy Griffith and Mount Airy. Thanks for buying this book. As Andy would say,

"I appreciate it, and good night."

Title page photos are of Andy Griffith and his parents Carl and Geneva Nunn Griffith on June 1, 1957, Andy's 31st birthday on "Andy Griffith Day" in Mount Airy for the movie premiere of A *Face in the Crowd*. Courtesy of the Winston-Salem Journal.

Citations for Recipients of the 2005
Presidential Medal of Freedom
Andy Samuel Griffith

Andy Griffith is one of America's best-known and most beloved entertainers. After his introduction to a national audience as a stand-up comedian on The Ed Sullivan Show in the 1950s, he went on to star in such celebrated television shows as The Andy Griffith Show and Matlock. As a legend of the stage, cinema, and television, Andy Griffith has built an enduring career and set a standard of excellence in entertainment. He is a man of humor, integrity, and compassion. The United States honors Andy Griffith for demonstrating the finest qualities of our country and for a lifetime of memorable performances that have brought joy to millions of Americans of all ages.

You can view the ceremony online at
http://www.c-spanvideo.org/program/189856-1

"Here at the White House, we get an interesting mix of visitors. Already today, I've met with the Secretary of State, Secretary of Defense, and the Dalai Lama -- and the Sheriff of Mayberry. Andy Griffith first came to the people's attention with his gift for storytelling -- and his own life is a mighty fine story by itself. He started out as a high school teacher, and in his amazing career, he has gained fame as an actor, and received a Grammy Award for his singing. He will always be remembered for *The Andy Griffith Show* and *Matlock*. Yet, he has also given powerful dramatic performances in such movies as 'A Face in the Crowd.'

Looking back on his Mayberry days, Andy explained the timeless appeal of the show. He said, 'it was about love. Barney would set himself up for a fall, and Andy would be there to catch him.' The enduring appeal of the show has always depended -- and still does -- on the simplicity and sweetness and rectitude of the man behind the badge. TV shows come and go, but there's only one Andy Griffith. And we thank him for being such a friendly and beloved presence in our American life."

-- President George W. Bush at the White House, November 9, 2005

Russell Hiatt, who started the Mayberry effect in Mount Airy shown here in the 1980s.

Contents

Every generation learns the magic of *The Andy Griffith Show* anew during Mayberry Days in Mount Airy as Wyatt Markwith did in this picture.

Introduction: Joy

Every year on the last Saturday in September, around nine in the morning, the hometown of the "Happiest Girl in the Whole USA," Donna Fargo, becomes the happiest town in the whole USA. Crowds descend upon Main Street in Mount Airy, North Carolina, on that day to watch the Mayberry Days parade. The look of joy on the faces of everyone present is something that I look forward to every year. I never laugh more or feel better about the place I live than on that day.

My grandfather lived a few blocks down Pine Street and occasionally reenacted Otis Campbell's intoxicated walk from the pool hall. I met him when present and helped him home. For this, I received a John Kennedy half-dollar piece. I recently relived some of my youth when Todd and Betsy Harris, who now own the home my grandparents lived on Pine Street, let me visit their home. I sat in the front window where I used to sit and read, looking at the big pink house across the street, and it brought me joy to revisit my own history.

I have revised this book for the sixtieth anniversary of *The Andy Griffith Show's* premiere by adding new photos and stories about the real town that is more like Mayberry than any other. This book is about Andy Griffith and his hometown. It has been my bestselling book and has brought me more joy than any other book I have written. Joy is what it is all about in Mayberry, and I, too, feel it when I think of Mount Airy.

I expect most people who come to Mount Airy searching for Andy Griffith or Andy Taylor, and the Mayberry experience love every moment of their encounter as well. Growing up, I thought everyone's hometown had a television show about it. Mount Airy is a great place to be from, but it is not just Mayberry.

For me, Mount Airy is the place I first bought a record, one 45 rpm single of The Beatles' *"All You Need Is Love/Baby You're A Rich Man"* at Dickson's Record Shop on Franklin Street. It is

11

the first place my mother bought me the Beatles' album *Let It Be*, which became one philosophy I [picked up from her for my life.

Mount Airy is the first place I sold a book, over a decade ago, at Talley's Custom Frame Shop, a relationship that continues at the Autumn Leaves Festival every October.

Mount Airy is the first place my father and I got a suit of clothes. Flip Rees gave my father his first suit because he thought the athletes, who represented Mount Airy High School, should look presentable when they traveled. My father never bought a formal piece of clothing anywhere else for the rest of his life.

Mount Airy is the first place my mother took me to Roses, which is the Mayberry Antique Mall today, to buy a model car of a 57 Chevy, or the *USS North Carolina* battleship, and she took me across the street to eat lunch in the Wolfe's Den, which is Bear Creek Fudge today.

This book has been a joy to my life because many people have told me how much they enjoyed it. This edition more than doubles the original size and adds much more information about Andy Griffith and his hometown, along with the many connections of the man and the town to the fictional town of Mayberry.

In late May 2014, I found myself watching *The Sixties*, a documentary on CNN produced by Tom Hank's Playtone production company. There were behind scenes clips and scenes of Don Knotts winning his many Emmy Awards for playing Barnie Fife. Knotts said, "Whether it is a situational comedy, a western, or a drama, it is the quality of the show itself that is important." The talking head in the show described Mayberry as a "kinder, gentler place" and mused, "Who would not want to live in Mayberry?" He continued that the core of the show was "this rock," Andy Taylor's character. Andy Griffith is heard saying, "I have taken the best parts of myself and people I that have known all my life and put them into Andy Taylor." They also discussed how people appreciate emotional honesty more than comedy, and when you

12

can do both as *The Andy Griffith Show* often did, that is rare in a sitcom and shows amazing depth. It was simply great storytelling.

The next few pages highlight some of the people who helped me with this book and make Mount Airy a wonderful place to live and visit if you are searching for Mayberry. A CBS executive once said, "What's better than giving families the opportunity to watch something pure, joyful, and wonderful? Who doesn't want to be in Mayberry?"

Julie Marion Brinkley, who lets me set up in front of her store, Mayberry Market and Souvenirs, during Mayberry Days, and watch the parade with her father, James Marion, a raconteur, reminds me of my father. Julie was one of the first merchants to embrace Mayberry in her business, beginning in 1991.

Below, people like Paul and Vickie Riekehof make a great
burger and share three grandsons with this author.

Here are some of the Mayberry Memories this book has given me. Coach Frank Beamer liked my book, as did Mayberry in the Midwest, who allow me to come each year.

R. Wayne Jones of Aiken, South Carolina, shared stories of his mother, a student of Andy Griffith at Goldsboro High School in Wayne County, North Carolina. Here Wayne is reading a book by this author about himself in Pigeon Forge, Tennessee, as he portrays my boyhood hero J. E. B. Stuart as he did all over the country.

Charles A. Brintle, my old Civil War Buff buddy from Yadkin County, North Carolina, who is holding a proof of this book, told me the story of his maternal grandfather Floyd A. Kidd, who worked at the Mount Airy Furniture Factory, who bought a Coke from Andy Griffith, who was selling them from a wooden tray in the same factory Carl Griffith worked for years.

18

Tribute artists David L Browning, Michael Oliver, Jeff Branch, Phil Fox, Alma Venable, Sandy Pettigrew, Kenneth Junkin, Allan Newsome, and Keith Brown are shown here in Westminster, South Carolina in 2013. Below, Christie McClendon, with the author, reminded me of the adage, "What Happens in Mayberry stays in Mayberry."

I had a memorable weekend once in Westminster, South Carolina, during Mayberry Comes To Westminster, when Maggie Peterson, "Charlene Darling" sat beside me most of the day on Saturday. She still sings "Salty Dog" and was a joy to talk to.

David Browning, "The Mayberry Deputy," made me laugh so much at Westminster, South Carolina that I helped him publish his autobiography, *"We Have Extra Security Tonight."*

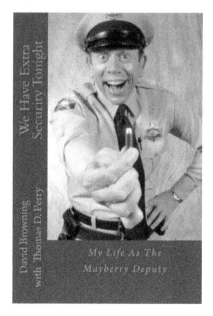

**This book brought me an invitation to the Virginia
Festival of the Book to talk about *Beyond Mayberry* in 2013.**

This book brought me the joy of having stories about it in
regional newspapers such as the *Greensboro News and Record*
December 23, 2012, shown on the next page.

The man, the town, the legend

Andy Griffith admirer travels down memory lane

By Jo Maeder
Special to the News & Record

"I was born in the Northern Hospital of Surry County, North Carolina," writes Thomas D. Perry, "just down the hill within sight of the home where Andy Griffith spent most of his time growing up and where he returned in 2002 to spend the night before Highway 52 became The Andy Griffith Parkway."

Perry is a historian and historical preservationist. He was born in 1960, the same year "The Andy Griffith Show" debuted.

Reared and still living in Ararat, Va., only 10 miles away from Mount Airy, he's also the owner of Laurel Hill Publishing. Perry has written, edited or published 33 books on this region's history.

"Beyond Mayberry: A Memoir of Andy Griffith and Mount Airy, North Carolina" is partly a memoir, partly a four book of Mount Airy (about an hour from Greensboro), and partly an extensively researched biography of his hometown's most famous native son. Griffith died on July 5, in Manteo.

Perry spoke about the book and his affection for Andy and Mayberry in a recent interview.

You say Andy Griffith never said for sure that Mayberry was based on Mount Airy. His eager reply when asked was, "It sure sounds like it, doesn't it." Could you address the controversy over where the "real" Mayberry is located?

In Jerry Bledsoe's book about biking the Blue Ridge Parkway, he talks about visiting the Mayberry Trading Post (in Mayberry, Va., 22 miles northeast of Mount Airy) and Addie Wood, the owner, telling him about Andy visiting the place as a kid. In Andy's papers at UNC-Chapel Hill he had a photocopy of the related pages and the paragraph I mentioned above was circled without comment.

You can read into that maybe that Andy was pleased to see that. I think his visits to Mayberry, Va.,

WANT TO READ IT?

"Beyond Mayberry: A Memoir of Andy Griffith and Mount Airy, North Carolina" by Thomas D. Perry (Laurel Hill Publishing, 214 pages, $19.99 paperback)

were a pleasant memory of his youth with his mother's family from Patrick County, where his mother, Geneva Nunn Griffith, was from, but that is just my opinion.

What do you think are the general public's biggest misconceptions about Griffith?

I think many people assume that Andy Griffith was Sheriff Andy Taylor. He was not.

I came to believe that Andy Taylor was Carl Griffith, Andy's father, who was a great storyteller and who Andy's first wife said was "the funniest man I ever know" — and she was married to Andy Griffith. Andy Griffith was a serious actor and he was playing a role. In real life, he was not as approachable as the character he played.

See Griffith, Page H5

BILL RICKARD
News & Record

Greensboro News and Record December 23, 2012

BOOKS

Griffith

Continued from Page H6

You wrote this book while recovering from surgery for prostate cancer that has some side effects, while generally temporary, that could throw any man into a depression. How did writing help you through that time?

I had surgery in February 2012 and, when Andy Griffith died in July, I was struggling to start work again.

Thomas Perry

I used the laughter from the show to heal, but it was a subject that I knew and that made it easier to write about something so close to home for myself, too. Prostate cancer for men is not easy, but I had robotic surgery (at Wake Forest Baptist Medical Center) in Winston-Salem and I'm now almost fully functional again.

"The Andy Griffith Show" has proven to be a timeless classic for all ages. Why?

"The Andy Griffith Show" was one of the funniest shows ever on television, especially when Don Knotts was on it. I think Andy took Mount Airy with him into the show and that made it real. Part of the appeal of the show is that it is taken from real life.

What were the most unexpected discoveries you made about yourself and Andy Griffith while writing or promoting "Beyond Mayberry"?

"The thing about Andy that I did not realize was how much a product of his parents he became. He got his musical ability from his mother's side and his storytelling from his father Carl, and probably the acting.

"As for myself, I was surprised at how much pride I began to feel for being from the same place as Andy Griffith. He received a Medal of Freedom from President George W. Bush and, if you look at the ceremony, you can see the joy Andy Griffith had in his face. It is the first thing in the book because I don't think we will see anyone from Mount Airy getting one of those again any time soon and I came to feel what a memorable event that was for Andy Griffith and Mount Airy."

"Beyond Mayberry" is loaded with such details as a mention of a birthmark on the back of Andy's head that his mother called "Andy's strawberry patch." And that he swept buildings for $6 a week to buy his first trombone. You also delve into his parents' and grandparents' past. You pored over old records in libraries and courthouses. Had this book been marinating inside you for a while?

It had been on my mind

"Beyond Mayberry" contains many photographs, including this one of barber Russell Hiatt in front of his Mount Airy barber shop. In the 1960s, Hiatt decided to promote his shop as Floyd's City Barber Shop, taking the title from "The Andy Griffith Show," and thus launched the cottage industry that Mount Airy enjoys to this day, according to author Thomas Perry.

for a long time since I found the marriage certificate of Andy's parents in the Patrick County, Va., courthouse. When he passed in July, I escalated my efforts. This book was easy to write as I grew up near Mount Airy and, like most people my age, Andy was part of my life from as long as I could remember. The reception of this book has been amazing.

Sequels

Continued from Page H6

embraced by teen readers for her previous books, including "Scorpio Races." Main character Blue has been told that she will cause her true love to die.

She stands every year with her clairvoyant mother as the "soon-to-be-dead" walk past. Usually she just accompanies her mother, but this year a boy appears to hear and speaks. He is Gansey, a rich student at a local private school.

And so Blue is drawn into the world of the Raven Boys at the school. Not a sequel.

Other series fiction that are worth a look if your teen has been reading titles by these authors in the past include:

• "Mark of Athena" by Rick Riordan (Hyperion)
• "Last Apprentice: Lure of the Dead" (Book 10) by Joseph Delaney (Greenwillow)
• "Enchantress: The Secrets of the Immortal Nicholas Flamel" by Michael Scott (Delacorte)
• "Last Guardian" by Eoin Colfer (Hyperion), the eighth and final Artemis Fowl book.

Nonfiction titles with a historical bent were plentiful this year. More are...

The first copy of *Beyond Mayberry* sold in Mayberry on Main in Mount Airy with owner Darrell Miles on the right. Below, my cousins Robert and Madison Pennington, from Georgia.

My late cousin, Adam Pennington, and his son, Adam, reenacting Andy and Opie going fishing.

In June 2013, I started my new career as a Darrel Miles Tribute Artist, continuing in the tradition of the many people who come to Mount Airy for Mayberry Days every September. Darrel and Debbie owned Mayberry on Main until 2019, which was where this book debuted in September 2012.

July 3, 2012

He was eighty-six years old on the morning of July 3, 2012. Early that morning, his heart stopped beating, and Andy Griffith passed away. He died at his estate on Roanoke Island along Highway 64/264, about 330 miles from his birthplace in Mount Airy. We will never know what his last thoughts were, but we would like to think that it was of home, the place he made famous as Mayberry on *The Andy Griffith Show* for eight years on CBS. North Carolinian Thomas Wolfe wrote that "You Can't Go Home Again," but Andy Griffith never really left Mount Airy, and he carried his hometown to the world.

When I think of *The Andy Griffith Show*, I think of peanut butter. Before I could drive and get a "real job" as a teenager in Mount Airy, I remember getting off the bus from high school around 4 p.m. in Ararat, Virginia. After petting Susie, my collie dog, the first thing I went for was a peanut butter sandwich wither with or without grape, strawberry, or apple jelly.

Relaxing on the couch with a big glass of my mother's powerhouse sweet tea and the sandwich mentioned above sometimes involved watching an episode of *The Wild Wild West* or *Gomer Pyle U.S.M.C.* from WFMY, channel 2, out of Greensboro and delivered to me on the antenna high above my parent's home before cable and satellite.

A couple of hours after school might include basketball with the neighbors or mowing the grass, but every afternoon included at least a half hour of *The Andy Griffith Show* with Andy, Opie, and especially Barney, usually between 5:00 and 6:00. There was nothing funnier on television in my youth than Don Knotts playing the clown to Andy Griffith's straight man. I always thought Andy Griffith looked bored after Knotts left the show to make movies.

My mother arrived home from her job of thirty-eight years shipping golf shirts for Quality Mills later, Cross Creek Apparel, to

27

make dinner for my father and me. The former tried to play golf every afternoon after a day, either teaching or being principal at Red Bank, then Blue Ridge Elementary School. My parents, like several others I came to know later, met while my father was in the U. S. Army, stationed at Fort Gordon, just outside my mother's hometown of Augusta, Georgia. They met at a barbeque place in the downtown of the Peach State's Garden City. My father's family came from a small town about an hour west of Chattanooga, Tennessee, where my father was born at the end of 1931. The Perrys, two sets of them, Uncle John and his nephew, another Erie, and my grandfather, came to Mount Airy, North Carolina, in the 1940s.

I was born in the Northern Hospital of Surry County in Mount Airy, North Carolina, just down the hill and within sight of the home where Andy Griffith spent most of his time growing up and where he returned in 2002 to spend the night before U. S. Highway 52 became The Andy Griffith Parkway. Andy Griffith became Sheriff Andy Taylor on October 3, 1960, exactly one month and one day before I was born on November 4.

I grew up in Patrick County, Virginia, where Andy's mother, Geneva Nunn Griffith, also grew up near the Dan River's waters, a few miles from the Ararat River, where I grew up. Patrick County never felt like home to me. Mount Airy felt more like home, but it was not where I grew up. Mount Airy was home to me because my father spent his later teen years there, and my grandparents lived there after moving from Tennessee.

Haymore Baptist Church was why we went to Mount Airy every Sunday, and sometimes we went on Wednesdays to be an RA, a Royal Ambassador. The RAs was a program for children that made us ambassadors for Jesus Christ in what was the second Baptist Church and named for a pastor with the name of Haymore. Andy Griffith also attended Haymore Baptist Church and grew up on Haymore Street, just a few blocks south.

Andy Griffith made his way to the Grace Moravian Church when the pastor encouraged his musical and comedic talents. Sort of like how I made my way to my paternal grandparent's apartment on West Pine Street in the Graves House after Sunday School, avoiding the regular 11:00 a.m. service. Looking back on it, I loved Sunday School because it was all about history.

History is what it is all about for me, and this book is part memoir, my history, and part biography, Andy Griffith's history, and the town we both share along the Virginia/North Carolina border. I saw Andy a few times, but I never met him. Like many, I feel he has been part of my life.

Not only did I share Haymore Baptist on Rockford Street with Andy Griffith, I realized that we were both only children who discovered music to escape the doldrums and loneliness of childhood. I spent one hot summer working in a tobacco field to buy a $100 Yamaha guitar from Easter Brother's Music Shop in Mount Airy. Unlike Andy, who swept outbuildings for six dollars a week to purchase a trombone, I did not have to leave Haymore Baptist Church and go across town to find a teacher. I found church member Sam Dobyns, who spent many hours teaching me chords to 1974 albums such as Ringo Starr's *Ringo* and Paul McCartney's *Band on the Run*.

The idea to author this book came to me one rainy day in April 2012, while I was recovering from prostate cancer surgery. The word cancer to a 51-year-old man, who has been humbled by the aftereffects, gives him time to pause and think about his life. My mind wandered to the happy days I spent with my grandparents in their apartment just a few houses down from the Mount Airy Library, which was in Kochtitzky House.

All of that came full circle on July 3, 2012, when word reached Mount Airy that Andy Griffith died early that morning on Roanoke Island on the Atlantic Coast, where he lived most of his adult life. Soon news came that the most famous man from the town at the foot of the Blue Ridge Mountains would remain along the coast, instead of coming home to rest in Grace Moravian Church Cemetery as many hoped when Andy had rejoined the church several years previous. The idea of Graceland and Grace Moravian was not to be.

My father's family was my connection to Mount Airy and the only encounter between the "two legends" in my life, Andy and my father. My father grew up a poor boy in Mount Airy. I found many parallels in the lives of the two men who met that day across the street from where I was born.

I found myself strangely emotional about it. Earlier in the day, I went to tell my father that Andy Griffith was dead. He did not know as he was lost in an old movie on Turner Classic Movies. A love of the movies he passed on to his only son. We spoke a few minutes about Andy. My father, who was halfway through his eightieth year on the day Griffith died, had gone to the same high school as Griffith but was a few years behind him and did not know him. They did have much in common, though, especially growing up in Mount Airy, and I always think of them together when I ponder the subject.

In 1966, before I started school, my father, Erie Meredith Perry, stood in line one day at the Hospital Pharmacy across Rockford Street from the Northern Hospital of Surry County. My father recounted this story to me on July 3, 2012, the day Andy Griffith died. The pharmacist Bob Smith looked up and said, "Well, Hello Andy." My father realized that Andy Griffith was standing in line with him, and neither one of the "legends in their own time or minds," as my father said, spoke to each other. I have never known my father to be without words in the fifty-plus years I have known him, but Andy was not in a speaking mood that day.

I fell for one of my father's verbal traps that July afternoon. When I asked him why he did not speak to Andy Griffith, my father replied that he was surprised to see Mount Airy's most famous son standing there in line with that he was speechless. I asked my father why Andy did not speak to him, and the trap was sprung. My father told me, "Well, son he was so amazed to have 'Erie-sistible' standing in front of him that he too was speechless." A college coed had given my father, "Erie Perry from Mount Airy," the nickname of "Erie-sistible," as he was so charming to the ladies.

Andy Griffith was in the drug store on personal business, specifically to have his mother's medicine billed to him. This information was recounted to me under my book tent at Pilot Mountain's Mayfest the following year by the then owner of the Hospital Pharmacy in 2013. It was probably this sort of thing that led Andy Griffith to move his parents, Carl and Geneva Nunn Griffith, to California in 1966, to be closer to their only son.

On the afternoon of July 3, the same day he died, Andy Griffith was laid to rest on the coast, the clouds opened on Mount Airy as if the sky was crying over the loss of its favorite son. I found myself watching the television coverage, and later, episodes on WFMY of *The Andy Griffith Show*, where I had first watched Jim West, Gomer Pyle, and Andy Taylor.

After years of speaking on J. E. B. Stuart all over the country, whenever I said I was from Mount Airy, the next thing people always said to me related to Andy Griffith or Mayberry. As a boy, I remember walking up Pine Street to Main Street in Mount Airy and having a hot dog at the Snappy Lunch with my grandmother or watching my grandfather get his hair cut next door in the City Barber Shop, now Floyd's City Barber Shop. Later, I took a class in Appalachian Studies at Virginia Tech. The professor could not say enough dreadful things about Andy Griffith. Her thesis was that every known stereotype to make Southerners look stupid was on display in the show and that he was cutting them with such a sharp knife they did not even feel it. I wonder what she would think if she could see the plethora of tourists who visit every year for Mayberry Days.

It is easy to criticize those who promote the idea of Mayberry, but for them, it represents the wholesome, nostalgic, and sanitized feelings they hope our hometown will have. Mount Airy is trying to become like Hannibal, Missouri, where boys like Tom Sawyers and girls like Becky Thatcher roam the street, bringing Mark Twain's writings to life.

Like Hannibal, where Huck Finn and African-Americans are virtually ignored, there are only white faces in Mayberry with few exceptions. It is not a real place with real problems. Sheriff Hudson Graham of Surry County once said, "We're not exactly Mayberry, but then in many ways we are. Folks come here with their problems, just as they do to Andy Griffith. Only thing, his writers are better at contriving happy endings than we can manage."

For many of his fans, Andy Griffith was the ultimate television father. In real life, he admitted he was not as good a father as Andy Taylor, but as for a good example of fathers and sons to follow, you could not ask for a better relationship than that Andy and Opie Taylor.

I was present when Highway 52 was named the Andy Griffith Parkway. Cagey as he was while playing Sheriff Taylor, Andy hinted that Mayberry was based on Mount Airy. He never confirmed it, but I have a theory. I imagine an actor in Hollywood in the early 1960s, working with others to develop the design for a show. The actor remembers as a young boy traveling with his father along the Blue Ridge Parkway, stopping in for a bottle of pop at a place called Mayberry. Shazam! This is my opinion and the history of the town where I was born and the most famous man's story to come from it. Thanks, Andy, for the entertainment. I appreciate it, and good night to you.

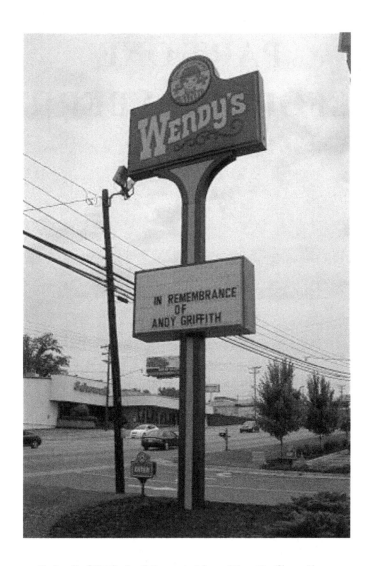

July 3, 2012, in Mount Airy, North Carolina.

PART ONE
BEFORE MAYBERRY

After losing his leg in the Civil War, Andy Nunn is shown sitting on the log with his crutch near a store in Claudville, Virginia.

Andy's Civil War

Following "Stonewall" Jackson was tough on many men during the War Between the States. The only way to avoid service was death, sickness, or a wound. Andrew J. Nunn of North Carolina found himself as part of the latter as his compatriots in the 21st North Carolina Infantry Regiment moved down to the peninsula between the James and York Rivers to fight with Robert E. Lee's Army of Northern Virginia in the summer of 1862.

Nunn found himself left behind at Mount Jackson, Virginia, in the Shenandoah Valley at the beginning of June 1862. Although Mount Jackson was not named for Thomas J." Stonewall" Jackson, who received his famous sobriquet "Stonewall" at the Battle of First Manassas as the Southerners called it. The Yankees called it First Bull Run when South Carolinian General Barnard Bee told his men to "Look at Jackson standing like a stone wall." The valley became famous for the exploits of Jackson, the former VMI professor.

Nunn received a wound at the First Battle of Winchester on May 25, 1861. The regiment lost twenty-one killed and sixty wounded. Serving under Richard Ewell's division in the brigade of Isaac Trimble, Nunn saw some hot action. One internet blogger described it this way. "Dawn of May 25th found Banks' forces defensively positioned on a range of protective hills just south of the town. Jackson launched assaults on both Federal flanks and immediately encountered fierce resistance." On the Confederate right, near the Front Royal road, Trimble ordered his "two Twenty Firsts" to charge a strongly positioned Union regiment. A member of the 21st North Carolina described the ensuing charge: "With a wild cheer, the regiment moved swiftly towards the enemy's line behind stone walls, and was met by a most terrific fire of infantry and grapeshot. The regiment moved right on to the stone wall, from which the enemy was pouring forth a perfect storm of canister and Minie balls from the right and left–cross-firing upon

35

us. Despite initially wavering in the intense fire, the Carolinians regrouped and joined their brothers in the 21st Georgia in driving the Federals from the field."

Nunn was one of thirteen wounded at Cross Keys and Port Republic culminating Jackson's Valley Campaign, one of the most famous military maneuvers in history. Andy Nunn recovered from his wound to fight on.

He had brothers in the war. Private Jefferson Nunn died at age twenty-four on September 25, 1861, at Thoroughfare Gap near Manassas, Virginia, of typhoid fever. Another brother, Private William H. Nunn, enlisted with his two brothers on June 13, 1861, and was present until October 1864.

The Nunns were part of the "Mountain Boys" that enlisted on May 29, 1861, in Danbury, Stokes County, North Carolina. The men traveled to nearby Danville, Virginia, where they became Company F of the 21st North Carolina Infantry Regiment (11th North Carolina Volunteers). The regiment included men from Davidson, Surry, Forsyth, Stokes, Rockingham, and Guilford counties.

Andrew Jackson Nunn was born on July 20, 1835, in the Brown Mountain section of Stokes County, North Carolina. He had eight siblings, William, Samuel, Ersula, Mary, Usley, Jacob, Martha, and Jefferson.

Andrew Nunn enlisted as a Private at age twenty-six. Other than being reported sick in October 1861, his early time in the war was not memorable. Eleven months later, his compatriots elected him 3rd Lieutenant on April 26, 1862. By June 1, he was in the hospital at Mount Jackson. He returned to duty and received a promotion to 2nd Lieutenant on August 28.

The area around Winchester was not a lucky place for Andrew Nunn. Two years later, as part of the 2nd Corps of the Army of Northern Virginia under General Jubal Early in Lewis's Brigade on July 20, 1864, he received a wound in the left thigh that broke his femur. Family tradition holds that he lost his leg. His luck ran out at Stephenson's Depot, when Union forces captured him. He spent the rest of the war in either federal hospitals or prisoner of war camps.

On May 9, 1865, Nunn was at Fort McHenry, Maryland, where Frances Scott Key received his inspiration to write the "Star Spangled Banner" five decades earlier. Union General Lewis Wallace, who later wrote *Ben Hur,* signed the order transferring Nunn from the General Hospital in Baltimore. On June 24, Nunn took the Oath of Allegiance and was released, ending Andy Nunn's Civil War. After the war, Andy Nunn married Louisa Anderson and moved to the Claudville/Red Bank area of Patrick County, Virginia. "An astute businessman, Nunn shipped dried apples, chestnuts, turkeys, chickens, and hams by wagons and oxen as far as Winston-Salem, North Carolina, as well as Danville and Norfolk, Virginia." He died in 1904.

Few references to the Civil War were mentioned on *The Andy Griffith Show* except for one memorable episode, "The Loaded Goat," from 1963. Sheriff Andy Taylor tells Mrs. Vickers, who called the Sherriff's office, assured that the blasting she hears out on the highway is not the Yankees attacking Mayberry. He assures her that the South is still holding on to Richmond, Virginia, the Capital of the Confederates States of America. Years later, the daughter of Andy Nunn's younger brother, Samuel, named her only son after these two Nunn brothers. Geneva Nunn called him Andy Samuel Griffith.

The grave of Andy Nunn in Claudville, Virginia.

Civil War General J. E. B. Stuart was born just outside Mount Airy in Patrick County, Virginia, where Andy Griffith grew up. This author led the effort to save part of Stuart's Birthplace, the Laurel Hill Farm, in the early 1990s.

Mayberry Trading Post along the Blue Ridge Parkway in Patrick County near Meadows of Dan and Mabry Mill.

Mayberry Presbyterian Church is one of the rock churches made famous by Reverend Robert Childress shown below and featured in *The Man Who Moved A Mountain.*

Dale Yeatts welcomed Betty Lynn, who played Thelma Lou on
The Andy Griffith Show, **to the Mayberry Trading Post in 2009.**
Ms. Lynn graciously signed the photo of their meeting along
the Blue Ridge Parkway in Patrick County, Virginia, on the
banks of Mayberry Creek and within sight of the Mayberry
Presbyterian Church.

Patrick County Virginia Connections

Several years ago, I found myself rummaging through the papers of the Patrick County Courthouse. As a lark, I looked up the last name Griffith, and there was a marriage license dated August 22, 1925, between Carl Griffith (1894-1975), a laborer, age 30, the son of John D. and Sallie Griffith of Mount Airy and Geneva "Nannie" Nunn (1899-1986), age 26, the daughter of Sam and Mary Jophina Cassell Nunn of Patrick County. The Reverend J. S. Rodgers of the Methodist South Church married the couple in Patrick County, probably in the town formerly known as Taylorsville, now Stuart, Virginia, on August 22, 1925. John Clark of the Circuit Court of Patrick County filed the document. Andy Griffith's mother grew up in a county where the county seat was called Taylorsville before it changed to Stuart in 1884.

Mary Jophina (Jopina or Jossina or "Jo Pinney") Cassell Nunn (1866-1938) was the daughter of Peter Cassell and Nancy J. Rogers. Samuel "Babe" Nunn (ca. 1850-1905) was the son of John (1802-1886) and Scenna Phillips Nunn. Andy Griffith's paternal grandparents were married on February 14, 1886, in Stokes County, North Carolina, and are buried at Old Hollow Primitive Baptist Church Cemetery in Mount Airy.

Geneva was born on May 26, 1899, at Meadowfield, Patrick County, Virginia. Today, the town is gone, but it was located where Highway 773, the Ararat Highway, crosses the Dan River on the Command Sergeant Major Zeb Stuart Scales Bridge. This author worked to get the bridge named for his neighbor, Scales, who was the most decorated non-commissioned officer to serve in the United States military from Patrick County.

Geneva's parents Peter Cassell (1830-1882) and Nancy Jane Rogers (1838-1888), lived in Patrick County. Peter descended from John Cassell (1798-1878) and Mary Polly Gilbert (1802-1903). John was Michael Cassell's son (1764-1826) and Mary Catherine Tobler (1769-1809).

43

Geneva's father, Samuel Robert Nunn, was born in the Brown Mountain section of Stokes County, North Carolina, in September 1852. Geneva had eight siblings, Jeffee, Minnie, William, John, Gracy, Flossie, Samuel, and James. Samuel Nunn died at Meadowfield on May 16, 1905.

Geneva's father, Samuel Nunn, owned 122 acres, nine miles from the courthouse. The family cemetery is located near Virginia Route 631 between Kibler Valley, where the Dan River rolls off the Blue Ridge and Fall Creek.

John Nunn descended from William Nunn (1756-1829) and Elizabeth Copeland (1758-1826). William's parents were John Nunn (1717-1786) of Surry County, Virginia, not North Carolina, and Phoebe Shelton. Peter Nunn (1689-1791) of Chesterfield, Virginia, and Elizabeth Burton Wharton (1694-1761).

Samuel Robert "Babe" Nunn ran a sawmill on Fall Creek, a tributary of the Dan River near where the Mount Airy and Eastern Railroad ran from Mount Airy to Kibler Valley in Patrick County, Virginia. When Geneva was young, Meadowfield was an industrial area along "The Dinky" Railroad. This author wrote a book about the railroad and gained much information from Colonel James Love of Patrick County. One story told to me by the late Colonel Love was that Andy's grandfather murdered a man and made a deathbed confession about it.

Fall Creek descends from the Blue Ridge Mountains before making its way to the Dan River near Meadowfield. If you followed the Dan River reversing the stream's flow up to the mountain plateau, you would find a small community named Mayberry. The center of the area is the Mayberry Trading Post, located there since 1858.

Mayberry was once the site of a general store, tannery, brickyard, barbershop, gristmill, and a post office first run by Confederate veteran Jehu Barnard of the 50th Virginia Infantry and later by others from 1872 until 1922. One family story tells that

44

Mayberry comes from a Colonel Charles Mayberry, a militia captain, who came into the area in 1809, but there were two Mayberrys, both named George in 1791 when Virginia cut Patrick County out of its eastern neighbor Henry County giving Virginia's first governor Patrick Henry the ability to see his name on a map.

Today, the Blue Ridge Parkway crosses Mayberry Creek and rolls by the Mayberry Trading Post just a few miles from Meadows of Dan, Virginia, and the famous Mabry Mill. Mayberry is also the home to one of the rock churches made famous by the Reverend Robert "Bob" Childress in the book *The Man Who Moved a Mountain*. It is the only Childress church in Patrick County, and the first one he converted from wood to rock.

Patrick County has a claim to be the "Real Mayberry." Jerry Bledsoe's book *Blue Horizons: Faces and Places from a Bicycle Journey Along the Blue Ridge Parkway,* published in 1993, tells a story from the time the parkway construction began. Addie Wood, of the Mayberry Trading Post, said Sam Nunn brought ginseng to the store to sell and sometimes brought along his grandson, a boy named Andy Griffith. Carl Griffith, Andy's father, was a visitor as well. Addie was sure that this Mayberry was the Mayberry on the television show. She said, "I'm confident that he did. His mother was raised within seven miles of here, and Andy's father, I know beyond doubt, came to the store here and brought him when he was just a little boy. Andy's mother told me that."

So, was Mayberry, Virginia, the inspiration many years later for the town's name on *The Andy Griffith Show*? Did it involve a good memory that a boy had of his maternal grandfather? As Andy might say, "It sure sounds like it, doesn't it?" In his papers at the University of North Carolina at Chapel Hill, Andy Griffith has a copy of Jerry Bledsoe's book with a giant star near the part about the Mayberry Trading Post.

The Mayberry Trading Post was the center of the community and served as the post office.

Jerry Bledsoe's book *Blue Horizons* tells Andy Griffith's story, as a young man, coming to the Mayberry Trading Post.

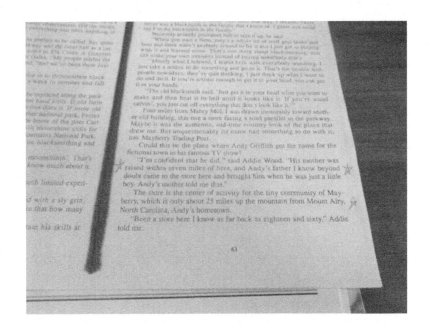

Among Andy Griffith's papers at his alma mater, UNC-Chapel Hill, is Jerry Bledsoe's book *Blue Horizon*, which is highlighted by Andy Griffith, leading this author to believe that Mayberry in *The Andy Griffith Show* comes from Mayberry, Virginia, as told to Bledsoe by Addie Wood shown below.

Cape Fear and Yadkin Valley Railroad.

Train with a load of Mount Airy Granite.

Mount Airy Depot, then and now in 2012.

SOUTHERN RAILWAY DEPOT, MT. AIRY, N. C.

The train station then and now in 2012, near the site of Andy Griffith's birthplace on South Street in Mount Airy.

Andy Griffith.

Double Birthdays in Mount Airy

The first train came to Mount Airy on June 20, 1888, and everything changed. Before that day, the sleepy town at the foot of the Blue Ridge Mountains was a place for growing tobacco and agricultural products. There was a giant outcropping of granite that many thought was useless, but the train changed that too as there would be a way to transport it out of the place that became known as the Granite City.

Before the train came, the Siamese Twins, Eng and Chang Bunker, walked the streets of Mount Airy before it became a city in 1885. Future Civil War General James Ewell Brown "Jeb" Stuart, who was born and grew up just across the state line in Patrick County, Virginia, also walked the streets of Mount Airy. Like people today from southwest Virginia, the Stuarts came to town for church, to pick up the mail, or to shop.

Several business people from the region in Virginia and North Carolina, including William and Jesse Moore, Winston and Joseph Fulton, Julius Gray, D. W. C. Benbow of Greensboro, A. T. Stokes of Richmond, Virginia, K. M. Murchison of New York City, Washington Williams, and E. J. Lilly of Fayetteville, Robert Gray of Raleigh, and W. A. Lash of Walnut Cove, North Carolina, wanted to link the beach to the mountains. The Cape Fear and Yadkin Valley Railroad rolled into Mount Airy for the first time after leaving Fayetteville at 8:00 a.m.

On that Wednesday morning, over 5,000 people were in town. A parade began on North Main Street and ended at the Rockford Street School site, where today, the Andy Griffith Playhouse is all that is left of the structure. The Governor of North Carolina, Alfred Moore Scales, a Democrat from Reidsville, was the guest speaker.

The train changed everything, giving a transportation route for the granite going out of the town. Soon furniture and textiles dominated the scene in Mount Airy, and the railroad was the highway to send all these products from Mount Airy to the world. The train station built around 1890 is now abandoned on Granite Street, one block from South Street. Within sight of the train station at 181 South Street, Dr. Thomas Worrell delivered Andy Samuel Griffith on June 1, 1926, ten months after his parent's marriage, but he did not get his name for six more days on June 7, 1926. He discovered that while he was born on June 1, his name was not registered until June 7, giving him double birthdays.

He was born in his paternal aunt's rented home that no longer exists on South Street in Mount Airy. The birthplace was a converted barn on South Street that the Griffiths shared with Geneva's sister, Grace, and brother-in-law, John Moore.

The blonde, blue-eyed, baby boy, Andy, slept in his aunt Grace Moore's bureau drawer in the rented house shared with her husband, John. The doting mother noticed her son had a birthmark on the back of his head. She called it "Andy's Strawberry Patch."

For those familiar with *The Andy Griffith Show*, you will be happy to know that when Andy was born in 1926, Calvin Coolidge was living in the White House. The quote from the 1964 episode "Aunt Bee's Romance" went like this.

Andy Taylor: "Well, as Mark Twain said, everybody complains about the weather, but nobody does anything about it." Floyd Lawson: "Did he say that?" Andy Taylor: "Mm-hmm." Floyd Lawson: "I thought Calvin Coolidge said that." Andy Taylor: "No, no, Floyd, Calvin Coolidge didn't say that." Floyd Lawson: "What'd Calvin Coolidge say?"

For a man known as "Silent Cal," Floyd thought the thirtieth President said many things. From another episode such as Andy: "Well, you know what Teddy Roosevelt said, 'Walk softly and carry a big stick.'" Floyd: "Oh, I thought Calvin Coolidge said that." Andy: "No, Floyd! Calvin Coolidge didn't say everything!" Floyd: "OH, I know what Calvin Coolidge said! 'I do not choose to run.'" Andy: "Well, yeah, he said that." Floyd: "I knew he had to say something, or he'd never got to be President. Are you sure that Teddy Roosevelt said, 'Speak softly and carry a big stick'?" Andy: "Yeah, he said that."

Andy's father, Carl Griffith, was a carpenter who worked in Mount Airy's furniture factories. His son described him as a "wonderful Christian man who had a strong influence on me."

Born in 1894, Carl Griffith served in the army from April 27, 1918, until January 5, 1920, which included World War 1. There are stories that he was gassed during the war and suffered from tuberculosis later in life, which included trips to a sanatorium in Winston-Salem, North Carolina.

Carl Lee Griffith was the son of John D. (1870-1938) and Sarah Frances Taylor Griffith (1872-1958). Andy's Griffith paternal grandparents are buried in White Plains Baptist Church near the Siamese Twins, Eng and Chang Bunker grave. Carl had six siblings: four sisters, Deanna, Jennie, Lena, Bertie, and two brothers, William and Edgar.

Yes, Andy had a grandmother surnamed Taylor, with the first name of Sarah. Sheriff Andy Taylor often talked to the town operator, Sarah, on the phone in Mayberry.

John descended from William Martin Griffith (1833-1895) and Charity Anne Childress (1834-1910). William's parents were Samuel Griffith and Polly Poor. Charity was the daughter of William and Fannie Vest Childress. Charity and William, "Andy Griffith's great-grandparents, were the generation to bring the family off the farm. Bill was a blacksmith in Mount Airy, leaving behind the land the family had farmed since Benjamin Griffith's land grant in 1786 south of town near Stewarts Creek."

Sarah Frances Taylor Griffith was the daughter of Henry Clay Taylor (1843-1900) and Rebecca Ann Simmons (1848-1943). Andy's great-grandparents Henry Clayton Taylor and Rebecca Ann Simmons were Quakers who lived in the Westfield community of Surry County from the early 1800s. They are buried in the White Plains Friends Cemetery.

Henry descended from Thomas George (1808-1870) and Sarah Ellen Boaz Taylor (1811-1877). Rebecca descended from Amos and Nancy Emily Inman Simmons.

Kate Rauhauser-Smith of the Mount Airy Museum of Regional History wrote a great article for *The Mount Airy News* in 2019 about Andy Griffith's genealogy. She wrote, "John Griffith, Andy's 4x great-grandfather, was settled in today's Surry County at least by 1772…Griffith served as an ensign of the first company of the militia through the colonists' war against the Cherokee and into the beginning of the Revolutionary War though he died before the Surry Militia deployed to Kings Mountain, Cowpens, or Guilford Courthouse.

John Newman, Andy's 4x great-grandfather on his mother's side, served in the Virginia militia throughout the Revolution and claimed bounty land in Patrick County as payment at the war's end. It was this family with others allied through marriage such as the Nunns, Phillips, and Cassels, who shopped at the big white building near the Parkway called Mayberry Trading Post."

In Terry Collin's book *Andy Griffith: An Illustrated Biography*, he writes that the Griffith Family left Mount Airy to live with Geneva's mother in Ohio. Gone for "roughly three years," the family moved to High Point, North Carolina, and eventually back to Mount Airy. My grandfather also moved his family from Tennessee to High Point and back to Chattanooga before settling in Mount Airy in 1949.

Upon returning to Mount Airy, the Griffiths lived in several places, including the Highland Park section on Huston Street, with Geneva's sister's family, and again on Rockford Street before buying a house on Haymore Street in 1935. In 1958, Andy Griffith renovated the house. He sold the property in 1966 to the Hale Family and moved his parents to California.

At age five, Andy's mother took him to his first entertainment, a production of *Carmen* in nearby Winston-Salem. The young boy was taken with the "clapping and clanging and carrying on!" of the production.

Griffith spoke of his parents in 1982, "Each of them gave me at least one special gift besides showing their love for me. My mother's family were all musical; they played guitars, banjos, fiddles, and other instruments. My father couldn't carry a tune, couldn't even whistle. But he had the best sense of humor of any man I ever met, and he was a great storyteller…my parents started off with two gifts right off the bat."

The Griffiths lived in a town that was very class conscious as most places were. The north side of town was where the men who owned the mills lived. Like my father's family, Andy Griffith lived on the south side of town, not south of the railroad tracks, but certainly within sight of the rails.

**Corner of Granite and South Streets in Mount Airy
near the site of Andy Griffith's birthplace, now torn down,
above and on the next two pages.**

The author's birthplace, the Northern Hospital of Surry County, which is just down the hill from the water tower that welcomes visitors and pictures Andy and Opie headed to the fishing hole across Haymore Street from Andy Griffith's Homeplace.

The author's father, Erie M. Perry, with his old friend Russell Hiatt in Floyd's City Barber Shop on August 29, 2012.

Old Hollow "Stewarts Creek" Primitive Baptist Church is the final resting place of Andy Griffith's maternal grandparents.

White Plains Baptist Church is the final resting place of both Andy Griffith's paternal grandparents and the Siamese Twins, Eng and Chang Bunker.

Graves of the Siamese Twins in White Plains.

Graves of John D. and Sallie E. Griffith in White Plains.

Andy's great-grandparents, Henry Clayton Taylor (1842-1900)
and Rebecca Ann Simmons (1848-1923), above.
Below, Charity Childress (1834-1910) and William Martin
Griffith (1833-1895).

Below, Mount Airy Furniture Factory, where Carl Griffith worked.

Two aerial views of downtown Mount Airy.

Growing Up On Haymore Street

The house located at 711 Haymore Street today cost Carl and Geneva Nunn Griffith $435. It was several blocks up a steep hill from the Mount Airy Chair Company, where Carl Griffith worked in various jobs as a mechanic and band saw operator making furniture such as dining room tables. He eventually reached a foreman's position before he retired at age 65.

Andy Griffith, and others, often talked about his father, such as Griffith's cousin Evin Moore who said, "His daddy was a great joker. There were never any dark moments with Carl Griffith." Andy's first wife, Barbara, said her father-in-law was "one of the funniest men she'd known." The apple did not fall far from the Griffith Family Tree.

Andy said of Carl Griffith, "I think my father had an enormous influence on me. He was a Christian man, truly honorable and honest, a fine human being, and he had a magnificent sense of humor…If he could've had a chance, he would've been a really fine actor.

He was the greatest foreman and band saw operator. He was a great father, much greater than I. He gave me everything. My sense of humor. My family values."

Carl was younger than most of the fathers in Mount Airy and was close to his son, Andy. Carl went to work at the age of twelve to offset his own father's gambling habit.

Geneva Nunn Griffith brought her Patrick County musical roots with her, and she taught her son to play guitar. You could say that Andy Griffith was on the Crooked Road, the Virginia Musical Heritage Trail, before anyone thought it up.

Andy heard gospel music at Haymore Baptist Church and then at Grace Moravian Church, along with the many tent revivals he attended growing up. People talked about how he liked the two pages in the Spiegel catalog that had musical instruments.

71

One particularly poignant story involves him walking downtown by himself to the florist and buying his mother a small potted plant, which was all he could afford. Geneva cried for three days over the kindness of her only child. Geneva pampered her only child. One contemporary said of Andy, "It seemed like he had everything."

Being an only child made Andy a target for the local bullies. Andy called it a "ceaseless battle against bullies." He said, "There were times when I thought I just wanted to die. I think I was driven to do the things I did so I could get out of Mount Airy."

Geneva invoked discipline on her son. He did not stay out late and knew what time to be home. He was not a kid that got dirty because he knew his mother did not want that sort of behavior. His contemporaries said Andy was too shy to skinny dip at the swimming hole at the Ararat River. They said he was a clumsy boy and not very athletic describing him as "all thumps," but they said he hit hard in football.

Growing up a working class lad in Mount Airy left scars on Andy Griffith. He did not often talk of those days, but in *Our State Magazine* in 2003 and other publications, he related some stories about his youth in the Granite City.

"Growing up in Mount Airy, we were poor people...All during the Depression, almost all the time, my father had a job somewhere. If our factory shut down, he would find one somewhere that was open. He was good at running a band saw, so he'd get the job."

In *Parade Magazine* in 1990, Andy said, "When I was real young, I didn't much like to work. I didn't like to pull a cross saw and throw wood under the house and things like that. What I did like was listening to *The Lone Ranger*. When I was working in a factory with my father, and I hated, working in the factory, work took up at quarter till eight, and we shut down at a quarter till five.

Now, *The Lone Ranger* came on at five, Monday, Wednesday, and Friday, and we'd just be draggin' along.

Finally, Dad would say, 'We'd better hurry up. We're gonna miss *The Lone Ranger*.' So, we'd sit together by the radio, and Dad would do something every time. When some character'd say, 'Who was that masked man?' 'Then the other person would say, 'That was the L-O-N-E Ranger,' and you'd hear, 'Hi Ho, Silver, Away!' My father'd go 'Whooooeee!'

Or, if something astounded him, or if he saw a really pretty woman, he'd do a whole body take, go 'Whooooeee!' and he'd walk out of the room and come back and do it again. Even now, periodically, I do a body take or make that sound, just like my dad did."

Rockford Street School near the Andy Griffith Playhouse's present location was the school's auditorium and the only building remaining. Andy repeated the fourth grade twice, not because the teacher liked him so much, but because of the myriad of childhood diseases he had caught, including the mumps and chickenpox. He was promoted to the fifth grade, but Miss Ruth Minick put him back in the fourth for another year with Miss Valentine. It was at this time one of his female classmates called Griffith "White Trash." When he got to high school, he was paired with that same girl as a monitor. With a smile, he described it as karma. Because of frequently moving, my father, too went through a grade twice.

"In school, I was the patsy that everyone picked on. They would hold me down and call me Andy Gump or Amos and Andy. And I hated, hated, hated it, but at some point, my child's mind recognized that I could control the kind of fun that was being made of me. In this way, it put me in charge of the laughter. So, I grew up as a class clown; it was a defense mechanism.

When I was a kid back in Mount Airy, North Carolina, the other fellas, and worse, the girls used to laugh at me. It seemed to me they laughed at me all the time. Not with me, mind you, but at

73

me. My mama made me wear long underwear, and when we had to change in the gym, the other guys would double over in hysterics. It finally got so I'd dress in the shower or toilet where no one could see me…I was awful shy, scraggly, homely kid…I wanted to belong like the rest of the kids, but I was embarrassed to express myself or my needs. I don't even think I knew what my needs were. There were times when I thought I wanted to die.

I guess it took me a long time to find out what I wanted to do. I always looked for a way to function as an individual person. But I started out a loser. Believe me. I was convinced I was born that way by the time I reached adulthood.

I wasn't smart, my family wasn't wealthy, and I wasn't athletic. If you aren't wealthy or athletic in a small town like Mount Airy, you aren't much. You know what I mean? I had to find something else for myself, something mine.

And it happened by chance to make something out of a handicap that so many people let pass by. One day I was a kid with a big hurt…and then I said something funny and made a whole room full of people laugh. They laughed at me, and all of a sudden, I was in control because I'd made them laugh.

That was a long time ago, but I've never forgotten the laughter. As long as everyone was going to laugh at me, anyway I might as well put myself in the position where I could control the laughter and turned a disadvantage into an advantage, and in doing it, I changed my whole life."

The event that changed Andy Griffith occurred on the stage of what is today the Andy Griffith Playhouse, when he was in the third grade. There are several versions of this story, but here is the first one. The person responsible was Albert McKnight, who sat next to Andy in homeroom. The teacher assigned Albert a poem to read representing their class in the Friday assembly. Andy sat on the aisle, and when the principal called for the next presentation, he stood up. Albert did not move. Andy found himself standing alone in the big room. "I walked up there on that stage."

In Andy's own words, here is what happened. "I don't know to this day what made me do it. I guess I was just plumb tired of being made a fool of. But I marched up to the stage and started reciting the poem we'd learned. In between the line, I'd make little comments of my own on what I thought of the poem and the person who wrote it, and they started laughing. I found out I could get them to laugh or listen whenever I wanted them to. What an experience, that great sea of laughter. From that time on, no one kidded me because they knew I could whip them verbally. And, most important, I knew it…A lot of us, most of us, I guess, had unhappy experiences as kids, and the secret is not to just overcome them, but to make the most of them. After all, experience is a dead loss if you can't sell it for more than it cost you."

There is another version. Andy and another student were to sing "Put On Your Old Gray Bonnet," but the other student did not show up. Griffith only knew the chorus, but that did not stop him. He sang the chorus slow and then fast.

*"Put on your old grey bonnet, With the blue ribbon on it,
While I hitch old Dobbin to the shay, And through the fields of
clover, We'll drive to Dover, On our golden wedding day."*

By singing it twice, Griffith caused the auditorium to erupt with cruel laughter. Griffith realized he was in control of the situation, and a star was born. He made triumph out of tragedy. No one messed with him in a war of words because he could "whip them verbally." He realized that laughter became his currency and was a source of self-protection.

Rockford Street in Mount Airy became Andy's neighborhood, from the school to the Methodist Church. There was football in the cow pasture on Granite Street. There was kickball on Broad Street.

Life at the corner of Rockford and Haymore Streets in the shadow of the giant water tower that today has the images of Andy and Opie Taylor going to the "Fishin Hole" was not entirely lonely. Andy grew up with a group of kids who remembered him whether he was building model airplanes or riding his bicycle all over town with his brown and white dog Tippy in a wire basket on the handlebars.

Douglass Benison, Garnett Steele, and Emmett Forrest recalled fond memories of growing up near Andy Griffith, and they remained his friends. They fished and played games like Kick the Can or told ghost stories at the corner of Rockford and Broad Streets with the other kids in the neighborhood. The kids played football across the street from Haymore Baptist Church and baseball on Reddic Field, where the City Hall is today.

Among his friends was James Kingsbury, who once rescued Andy from punishment by telling Geneva that some boys tied Andy up in the Old Tabernacle Church. He said that Andy's mother was "serious with no sense of humor with kids." She was pretty and well dressed. Carl Griffith loved to garden, made woodcrafts, and refinish furniture. James was the son of Anderson and Beatrice Kingsbury. Yes, his mother was named Bea, like Aunt Bea (Aunt Bee).

Kingsbury told of the days growing up in Mount Airy with Andy Griffith. It was a time when you played Rag Bag Ball, made kites out of sticks, newspapers, flour, water, and made the tails from sheets. Kids swam in Lovill and Stewart's Creek and roamed the streets in shooting out streetlights with slingshots. As Opie Taylor found out, a slingshot can get a boy in trouble when he killed the mother bird in a favorite episode of *The Andy Griffith Show*.

Kingsbury told of riding bikes down the steps of the Methodist Church on Rockford Street. There was a "Big Gulley" on Creed Street, where the boys rode limber trees down to the ground and built a fire to roast corn and apples. They played football in the churchyard and stole watermelons.

Another friend from Andy's youth was Thomas Garnett Steele. He told of building models of the USS *North Carolina* battleship with Griffith. The boys built a model city in Griffith's basement from blocks, including a model train set. This author remembers trips to Mount Airy to buy a model of the same ship downstairs at Roses on Main Street on weekly Saturday trips to town.

Andy saved his money to buy an Ocarina, a "Sweet Potato" pipe. Wikipedia says, "The ocarina is an ancient flute-like wind instrument. Variations exist, but a typical ocarina is an enclosed space with four to twelve finger holes and a mouthpiece that projects from the body. It is often ceramic, but other materials may also be used, such as plastic, wood, glass, clay, and metal." Steele showed up on the show *This Is Your Life* on March 25, 1971, when Griffith was the subject, much to Griffith's chagrin at first. Steele told of how he and Andy let the air out of some guy's tires, but they realized the guy was in the car at the fourth tire. They spent the rest of the evening pumping up the tires. Like all boys, Halloween pranks, such as letting the air out of car tires, were part of life. While Andy claimed not to remember doing that, Garnett Steele said, "He was a person who didn't want anything to take away from him, from his prestige."

The boys took blocks of wood from the furniture factory and made them into cars, trucks, and other toys, including model airplanes. "Under Andy's house, it was very dry, and we would build roads and play there when it rained. Our cars and trucks were made of wood his father used for kindling."

They played "King of the Mountain" in a big gully on Creed Street. There were persimmon wars, like snowball fights, and playing games of "Fox and Dog," a group hide and seek.

77

Andy Griffith grew up attending Haymore Baptist Church, the same church this author grew up attending, just a few blocks from Andy's home on Haymore Street, north on Rockford Street, where he joined the young people's group to do his "early courting."

While at Haymore Baptist Church, Andy Griffith accepted Jesus Christ as his Lord and Savior. He later recounted, "God has been part of my decision and the cause of my success." His Sunday School teachers were Ruth Gentry, Luther McMillian, Ruby Wagoner, Wheeler Gough, and Katherine Moody. His contemporaries Emmett Forrest and Bill Chandler attended Haymore too. Griffith was famous for singing *"Jesus Loves Me"* so loud and out of tune that people would turn and stare. He sang solos on hymns like *"Sweet Hour of Prayer"* and served as the bell ringer. At age eleven, he played a farmer in a Christmas play, which was his first time acting in public. This author remembers ringing that same bell to call people to the morning service at eleven o'clock and acting in the Christmas play.

Steele spoke of Andy's favorite food, the hot dog. The Blue Bird Café had the best hot dogs in town. Pete Owens, the owner, sold beer and would not let the kids eat where beer was sold, so they had to go outside to eat. The Snappy Lunch was usually crowded, and the owners were "strict on kids."

Griffith, in 2002, described getting a quarter from his mother. He spent ten cents on a movie and ten cents for a hot dog and a bottle of pop at the Snappy Lunch.

The back problems that would plague Griffith later in life occurred about this time. Floyd Pike, who became famous for his electrical company, was dating Emmett Forrest's sister at the time and put up a knotted rope for the boys to swing on. Griffith fell from it and hurt his back. Steele said, "I think that could be one of the reasons he was deferred from service" in the U. S. military.

The Graves House was my grandparents' home when this
author grew up just a block away from Andy Griffith's
birthplace on South Street. Today, it is the home of Todd and
Betsy Harris.

"CHRIST IS NOT ONLY NECESSARY, HE IS ENOUGH"

The Sunday School presents their annual
Christmas entertainment tonight, 7:30. The
program starts promptly at 7:30, so come
early and get you a good seat. The program
consists of the following:

Songs, recitations, dialogues, etc. by the
Primary, Junior and Intermediate departments
under the direction of Mrs. Pansy Shelton,
iss Doris Midkiff, and Mrs. Sam McKnight:
lso recitations from the Cradle Roll under
he direction of Mrs. Fred McKnight.
A Play by the adult department, "Christm
ith Aunt Cynthia" under the direction of
rs. Evan Moore.
The cast is as follows:

Haymore Baptist Church Christmas program from 1941 featuring Andy Griffith.

Mrs. Robert Parker---Miss Dora Welborne
Mr. Robert Parker-----Evan Moore
Bob Parker, the son---Harvey Wagoner
Mary Lou--Daughter--- Dorothy Norman
Aunt Cynthia--Spinister Aunt--Edith Midk
Josephus--Hired man---Andy Griffith
Grandpa Flemming------Albert McKnight
Grandma Flemming------Evelyn Brannock
Jane--Grandchild------Rita Ann Stevens
Roy---Grandchild-------Donald Midkiff
Ralph Reid--Banker-----Luther McMillian

The play opens in Chicago with the Parke
mily preparing to go to Clay Center for
ristmas. Clay Center, a down-state vill
the old home of Robert Parker and his w
ry, and it has long been their custom t

81

Haymore Baptist Church on Rockford Street was home to the Griffiths, who lived several blocks near the water tower, shown in this photo's distance.

Scenes from the interior of Haymore Baptist Church, where Andy Griffith first acted in the Christmas play.

Grace Moravian Church on North Main Street, where Andy Griffith met Reverend Mickey to get trombone lessons.

Trombone Lessons

"Woosh! Screech!" Before he saw him, he heard him, Reverend Edward T. Mickey Jr. recalled years later in an article for *The Wachovia Moravian*. The bicycle came to a fast and loud stop at the Grace Moravian Church's back door at the corner of North Main and Old Springs Road in Mount Airy, North Carolina.

It was a Wednesday in February 1942. Mickey had just finished teaching the "horn" to a group of a dozen children from his congregation. He wanted a "church band to play chorales for special services," but things were not going very well that day as the children were not interested, and the preacher expressed feeling a little down about the prospects.

That day the entire world was feeling a little down as World War II was in full fruition. In the Philippines, forces of the United States were fighting the Battle of Bataan against the Japanese. The British lost Singapore, which was considered the worst loss in the empire's history that once ruled the seas. The Soviet Union forces, our allies, pushed the German Nazi forces back from Kursk, signaling the end of their offensive in Russia. President Franklin D. Roosevelt signed Executive Order 9066, creating Exclusionary Zones on both coasts that would lead to the United States government placing citizens of Japanese descent into internment camps, questioning their loyalty to the United States.

Grace Moravian Church started in 1923 when Brother Charles D. Crouch began preaching. In April 1925, ninety-six people received baptism, and the cornerstone of the building was laid on September 13, 1925. In May 1929, Brother John Sprinkle took over preaching until 1933 when Reverend Mickey arrived.

In the summer of 1941, before the war came to Pearl Harbor, *Birth of the Blues* starring Bing Crosby and Mary Martin was released to moviegoers. Andy Griffith sat watching it in one of Mount Airy's downtown theaters when he saw the trombone player. He was hooked and began to save his money.

Andy claimed that Skipper Sims, who taught math and coached baseball in the Mount Airy schools, taught him to add, and he needed to add, to save the money for the horn.

Weldon Leo "Jack" Teagarden, considered by many to be the father of the jazz trombone, played "Big T" in the film, *The Birth of the Blues,* with a glass over the end of the instrument. He later played a town councilman on *The Andy Griffith Show.*

Andy said of his new interest in music. "My daddy couldn't afford it. He fed me and clothed me, but he couldn't stretch his pay far enough to buy me a musical instrument…I got the trombone, and I was the happiest boy in all North Carolina."

At age 15, Andy saved money by sweeping Mount Airy High School for six dollars a month to raise the thirty-three dollars for the trombone. It took him six months to raise the money. There was no band at the high school. A foreman at the furniture factory told Carl Griffith that Reverend Edward Timothy Mickey, the minister at Grace Moravian Church, was known for his brass bands.

This author remembers spending one incredibly sweltering summer in a tobacco field to save enough money to buy a guitar from the Easter Brothers in Mount Airy. Did Andy and this author have the same goal in mind? Girls! I think so.

"You the preacher here?" said the "rawboned boy of sixteen with curly, blond hair" sitting "astride" the bicycle as described by Reverend Mickey, who answered affirmatively. "You teach horn?" Again, Mickey answered positively, "inwardly groaning," while thinking, "O Lord, here's another one!"

Mickey took the initiative stating, "I teach the young folks here at the church." The boy replied, "You teach me? I'll pay you." Mickey replied he could not take pay for doing his job in the church and asked the young man, "Why do you want to learn to play a horn?" The boy replied, "So I can lead a swing band."

The conversation continued with Mickey knowing he was digging his hole deeper. "What kind of horn do you want to learn to play?" The boy replied, "Trombone." Mickey saw a way out of his conundrum. "I don't know anything about the trombone. All I could do would be to go through an instruction book with you."

"I got an instruction book," the boy replied. As if in a war of wits with his young antagonist, Mickey said, "You'll have to have a horn," hoping that since he did not see one, he could get out of this easily, but the boy responded, "I got a horn." "Where did you get it?" asked the preacher. "Spiegel's," responded the young man. Mickey gave up and said to the boy, "Well, come again next Wednesday and bring your horn. We'll see what we can do." Mickey thought to himself that the boy would not ride the bike two miles across town "for long to do this," but Edward T. Mickey, Jr., like many other people in Mount Airy, soon learned of the determination of Andy Griffith.

The following Wednesday, in February 1942, there was young Andy on a bicycle with a trombone. Griffith had ridden two miles across town and up Lebanon Hill. Mickey wrote, "...combined with enthusiasm for life in quantity enough for half a dozen boys," but he was still not convinced of Griffith's conviction. He did not want to buy instruction books until he knew for sure the young man was in it for the long haul.

Mickey sent Griffith home with a musical scale written on a piece of paper kept the trombone book to study himself. The next week Griffith came back with the scale "note-perfect," as Mickey recalled. He gave Griffith the instruction book with a lesson, and Andy returned the next week with his lesson "note-perfect. After three weeks, Griffith asked, "Is that all? I can do more." Mickey gave him two lessons, which Andy performed the next week, "note-perfect."

Reverend Mickey inquired of his young music student when he had time to practice, as Griffith's rapid progress took many hours to hone his skill. Andy Griffith responded, "Well, I tell you: I've got my schoolwork, and I've got my studying, and I've got my paper route, and I've got my church work. And that doesn't leave me much time, so I've been getting up about five o'clock in the morning to practice!" Mickey wrote, "My heart went out to the neighbors until I realized that the neighbors also got up about 5 a.m. to go to work."

Andy soon joined the band for rehearsals on Monday nights. His first solo was Beethoven's "Moonlight Sonata." During intermission at rehearsal, he took the time to learn the other instruments. Mickey wrote that he and the other band members got a bonus from Andy, "his zest for life and for what he was doing caught on with the rest. The whole group, and yes, the director also, came out of the doldrums, which had enveloped it."

For the next few years, the world would fight a war while Reverend Mickey and his new student continued their music and singing studies. Young Griffith did not like to sing in the choir at first, saying it was "too sissy," but soon, he could not "sing enough." Singing later helped pay Griffith's way through college, and one day Andy Griffith would win a Grammy Award for singing gospel music.

Andy credited his father, Carl, and his preacher, Mickey, for changing his life. The latter became concerned about Andy spending so much time away from Haymore Baptist Church, on Rockford Street, but soon the Griffith family joined Grace Moravian.

After joining Grace Moravian Church, Griffith talks about the Easter Sunrise Service that started at three in the morning. "We'd ride around on the back of a truck with our trumpets and trombones waking everybody up, and then we'd all go to the churchyard and just wait. And then, just as the sun started to crack, the preacher would come out of the church. He'd be all dressed in white, and everything would be quiet. 'The Lord has risen,' he'd say. 'The Lord has risen indeed.' And then we'd march to the graveyard and sing hymns. Some were quiet, and some were jubilant, but they were all beautiful."

In 1944, Reverend Mickey left Mount Airy for a congregation in Raleigh, North Carolina. That same year, when Griffith left for college, thirty guests, including the Youth Fellowship of Grace Moravian Church, met on a Tuesday evening to say goodbye to Andy. He was accepted as a candidate for the ministry by the Provincial Elders Conference of the Moravian Church South, which included four years at Chapel Hill and three years at the Moravian Theological Seminary in Bethlehem, Pennsylvania. "Andy sang several selections and played a trombone solo."

Andy said his time at the Moravian Church was the "turning point in my life…" Griffith said at high school, Miss Haymore "encouraged me to go all out for music." It "was the kind they used to make movies about."

The preacher followed his former student's career, and Mickey returned to Mount Airy in 1957 when Griffith's first movie, *A Face in the Crowd,* premiered on Andy Griffith Day, invited by the Chamber of Commerce. Reverend Mickey continued to contact Andy Griffith, visiting him in Manteo, North Carolina, or meeting him on Griffith's infrequent trips to Raleigh.

Years later, local educator and historian Ruth Minick wrote another story of the appreciation Andy Griffith had for the man who got him started in "show business." In a telephone conversation with Griffith, Mickey bemoaned that he did not have a fourteen-year-old boy to mow his grass. Time passed, and one day an "unkempt figure with cap and dark glasses appeared" at Mickey's door with a riding lawnmower on a truck. The Reverend Mickey told the man that he had not ordered a lawnmower. Mickey called the store and finally got the name of the person who ordered the lawnmower, Andy Griffith. When he returned to the door with his "birdshot rifle," surprising his deliveryman, Reverend Mickey found his deliveryman was Andy Griffith.

Mickey summed it up this way. "Through the years, Andy's generosity in referring to the Moravian Church and to me as having been a cherished part of his life, has been a source of much enjoyment and appreciation on the part of many of us who have known him. We should not take too much credit for this; it was Andy's doing. Had he not been what he was, and is, in basic character and goodness, he would have been just another of the many in his profession who have lost their ideals and sense of values. He lives under the pressures which the rest of us would find intolerable, and does so without sacrificing his own integrity and Christian character."

As alluded to earlier, life was not all fun and music for Andy Griffith growing up in Mount Airy. One of the jobs of the church band was cleaning the building. He made up songs, invoking the cloth donated from Spencer's Inc., a maker of children's clothing in Mount Airy, which was known for their light blue buildings that can still be seen downtown. Griffith would sing, "Wash your windows with Dr. Spencer's underwear."

He worked for his cousin Evin Moore at the Weiner Burger. Moore kept Andy busy mostly washing dishes, but he could make milkshakes, and he made, yes, that is right, hot dogs. It is the hot dog that runs through Griffith's life and not the pork chop sandwich. Griffith bagged groceries at the Piggly Wiggly on Oak Street after school to make money.

Andy became interested in girls. Eleanor Powell wrote in *The Mount Airy News* about Griffith's love life. "The year was 1944. The place was Mount Airy High School. The subject was Andy Griffith. He was a popular kid on the block with a musical background. He had a teenage girlfriend, and all the younger students loved to watch as he turned on the school water fountain for her to get a drink of water. As an eighth-grade freshman, I was fascinated with their courtship."

The object of Andy's desires was a girl named Angie Marshall. "We don't know exactly what Andy Griffith is always saying to Angie Marshall that makes her have that faraway look in her eye, but we can imagine that it is something like this, 'Whither thou goest, I will go.'" For three years, Angie was Andy's girlfriend."

Angie was the captain of the girls' basketball team. This led Andy to try out for the boy's team. He found himself as the third-string center. He got into games when Mount Airy was way ahead. In one game, Griffith told the story of one of his teammates throwing him the ball. He said he didn't know where that ball went. Coach Wallace Shelton demoted him, but in English class, Griffith tells of teacher Wallace Shelton having him read aloud a story Andy wrote about a rabbit hunt, which got him laughs, continuing to reinforce the idea that humor was his way out of Mount Airy.

Near the end of his career at Mount Airy High School, Robert Merritt, who went on to run Renfro Corporation in Mount Airy, recalled how "shocked" they were that Andy agreed to sing at the Senior Banquet. "In high school, Andy never attracted much attention as far as I can remember. Nothing in his manner suggested a career in acting, but about halfway through the program, Andy sang 'Long Ago and Far Away.' During a moment of stunned silence, someone expressed our surprise by exclaiming 'Gollee ol' Ange can sing.' Long and enthusiastic applause followed. He consented to an encore and another one…Years later, I was not surprised by his success on stage."

The monthly newsletter of the MAHS Journalism class stated, "At the senior banquet, many girls were swooning to Andy's singing of 'Long Ago.' To top this, some of the boys were too!" Another girl wrote, "The girls simply swoon when Andy

Griffith sings, I can't decide whether he is like Frank Sinatra or Nelson Eddy."

Andy graduated from Mount Airy High School on May 30, 1944, in the same auditorium that bears his name today. He is described in his annual as a Glee Club member and the Athletic Club, having played basketball. He liked music most and disliked work. "His second ambition is to have a wife and six children. He plans to enter the Navy next year." In 2005, Griffith said, "When I was in high school, I was not athletic, we didn't have money, and I was not a good student. But when music came into my life, with the trombone and the singing, I became somebody."

Reverend Edward T. Mickey, Jr.

The Steele Building near the Old Well at UNC-Chapel Hill was the home to Andy Griffith while in college, shown on this and the next page.

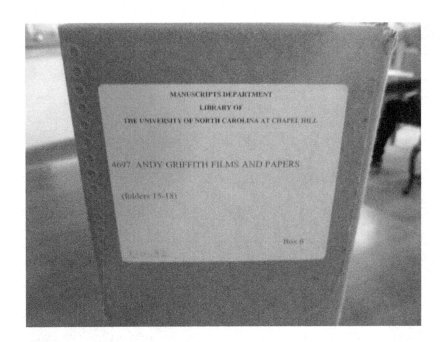

Andy Griffith's papers at UNC-Chapel Hill contain scripts from The Andy Griffith Show, including one of my favorites, "The Loaded Goat," shown here and on the next page, along with personal papers.

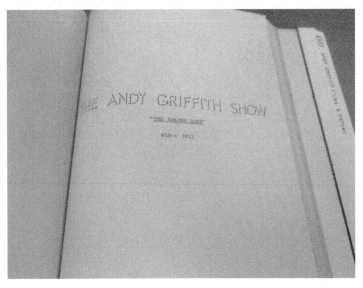

Andy Griffith with his parents, Carl and Geneva.

Marriage License

Virginia *Patrick County* to-wit:

To Any Person Licensed to Celebrate Marriages:

You are hereby authorized to join together in the Holy State of Matrimony, according to the rites and ceremonies of your Church or religious denomination, and the laws of the Commonwealth of Virginia,

Carl Griffith and *Geneva Nunn*

Given under my hand, as Clerk of *Circuit* Court of *Patrick* Co. (or *City*) this ___ day of *Aug.*, 1925

_____, C

Marriage Certificate

To be annexed to the License, required by Section 5074 of the Code of Virginia, 1919, as amended by Act of February 16, 1910.

VIRGINIA: In the Clerk's Office of the *Circuit* Court for the County (or City) of *Patrick*

Date of Marriage *Aug 22, 1925* Place of Marriage *Patrick Co.*

(FULL NAMES OF PARTIES)

Carl Griffith and *Geneva Nunn*

Age of Husband *30* years; Condition (single, ~~widowed or divorced~~) *single*

Age of Wife *16* years; Condition (single, ~~widowed or divorced~~) *single*

Race (White or ~~Colored~~) *white*

Husband's Place of Birth *Surry Co. NC* Mailing Address (PRESENT) *Mt. Airy N.*

Wife's Place of Birth *Patrick Co. Va.* Mailing Address *Mt. Airy N.*

Names of { Husband *John D. Griffith* and *Sallie Griffith* }
Parents { Wife *Sam Nunn* and *Josie Nunn* }

Occupation of Husband *Laborer*

Given under my hand this ___ day of *Aug* 19__

_____, C

Certificate of Time and Place of Marriage

I, *J S Rose*, a *Minister* of the *M.E. Ch.* Church, or religious order of that name, do certify that on the *22nd* day of *Aug*, 19__ at *Stuart*, Virginia, under authority of the above License, I joined together in the Holy State of Matrimony the persons named and described therein. I qualified and gave bond according to law authorizing me to celebrate the rites of marriage in the County (or City) of *Patrick*, State of Virginia

Given under my hand this *22nd* day of *Aug* 19__

_____
(Person who performs ceremony sign here.)

The Minister or other person celebrating a marriage is required, within thirty (30) days thereafter, to return the License and Certificate of time and his certificate of the time and place at which the marriage was celebrated to the Clerk who issued the License; failure to comply with these requirements the law makes the Minister or other person celebrating the marriage liable to a fine of not less than ten nor more than twenty dollars for each offense. Section 5074 of the Code of Virginia, as amended by Act approved February 16, 1910, Acts 1910, chapter 28, pages 36 and 37).

Marriage Certificate of Carl and Geneva Nunn Griffith discovered by this author in the Patrick County Virginia Courthouse in Stuart, Virginia.

North Carolina State Board of Health

BUREAU OF VITAL STATISTICS

STANDARD CERTIFICATE OF BIRTH

1. PLACE OF BIRTH

County _Surry_ Registration District No. _8C 2C 23_ Certificate No. _111_

Township _Mt Airy_ or Village _____

City _____ (No. _181 South_ St.: _____ Ward)
(If birth occurred in hospital or institution, give its name instead of street and number)

2. FULL NAME OF CHILD _Andy Samuel Griffith_ (If child is not yet named, make supplemental report, as directed)

3. Sex of child _male_ | To be answered only in event of plural births. | 4. Twin, triplet, or other _____ | 6. Parents married? _Yes_ | 7. Date of birth _June 9, 1926_

5. Number, in order of birth _____ | (Name of Month) (Day) (Year)

8. FATHER	14. MOTHER
Full name _Carl Lee Griffith_	Full maiden name _Geneva N. Nunn_
9. Residence (Usual place of abode) If nonresident, give place and State _Mt Airy_	15. Residence (Usual place of abode) If nonresident, give place and State _Mt Airy_
10. Color or race _white_ 11. Age at last birthday _36_ (Years)	16. Color or race _white_ 17. Age at last birthday _27_ (Years)
12. Birthplace (city or place) (State or country) _Surry_	18. Birthplace (city or place) (State or country) _Patrick Co Va_
13. Occupation Nature of industry _mechanic_	19. Occupation Nature of industry _Housewife_

20. Number of children of this mother (Taken as of time of birth of child herein certified and including this child.) (a) Born alive and now living _1_ (b) Born alive, but now dead _____ (c) Stillborn _____

21. Did you use drops in baby's eyes at birth to prevent blindness? _Yes_ If not, why not? _____

CERTIFICATE OF ATTENDING PHYSICIAN OR MIDWIFE*

22. I hereby certify that I attended the birth of this child, who was _alive_ at _3_ on the date above stated.
(Born alive or stillborn) (Hour a.m. or p.m.)

23. (Signature) _S. H. Worrell_
(State whether physician or midwife)

24. P. O. _____

Given name added from supplemental report

_____ 19_____

/ 25. Witness _____
(Signature of witness necessary only when 23 is signed by mark)

26. Filed _July 5, 1926_ 27. _J. C. Hill_
Local Registrar

Registrar

28. P. I. _____

*When there was no attending physician or midwife, then the father, householder, etc., should make this return. If a child breathes even once, it must not be reported as stillborn. No report is desired of stillbirths before the fifth month of pregnancy.

Birth Certificate of Andy Samuel Griffith.

Andy as a young man growing up in Mount Airy.

Andy in the seventh grade.

Andy with the band members from Grace Moravian Church.

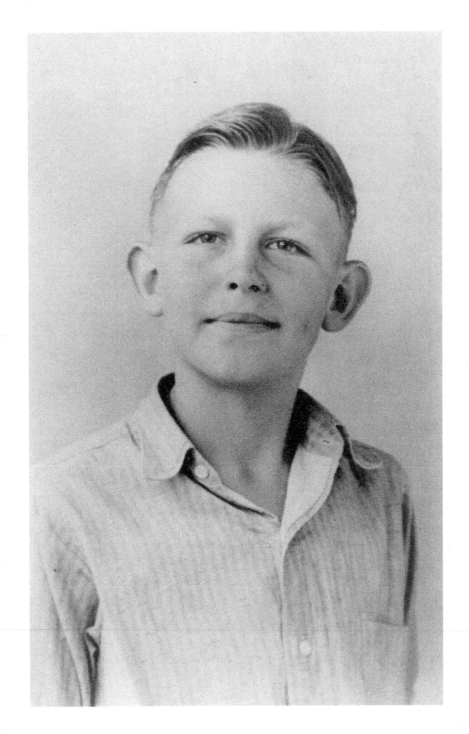

On the old farm-house ve-ran-da there sat Si-las and Mi-ran-da, thin-king of the

days gone by; Said he "Dea-rie don't be wea-ry, you were al-ways bright and

chee-ry But a tear, dear, dims your eye." Said she, they're tears of glad-ness, Si-las,

they're not tears of sad-ness; It is fif-ty years to-day since we were wed. "Then the

old man's dim eyes brigh-ten'd and his stern old heart it ligh-ten'd As he turned to

her and said:" Put on your old grey bon-net with the blue rib-bon

on it while I hitch old Dob-bin to the shay; Through the fields of

clo-ver on the way to Do-ver on our Gol-den Wed-ding Day.

Rockford Street School.

Andy Griffith, back row center, fourth from the left wearing glasses.

"That boy sure did have a good head of hair." The following pages show that, and he had it until the day he died.

Above, Andy Griffith's World War Two Draft Card. He did not serve due to a bad back

Many people come to Mount Airy each year looking for the simplicity of Mayberry. The statue of Andy and Opie Taylor going to the fishing hole represents many things, such as one of the greatest father/son relationships of television.

Beyond Mount Airy

Andy Griffith left Mount Airy in 1944 to attend the University of North Carolina at Chapel Hill. He planned to become a Moravian preacher, which made him exempt from military service. The exemption did not sit well with some back home, but Andy also had back problems that kept him from the service. Griffith had a herniated disk in his lower back from an injury at age thirteen when he fell from a tire swing in Emmett Forrest's yard. Andy did not need to be a minister to get out of military service. Andy felt immense pride in his accomplishments, as he was the first in his family to attend college. Again, this parallels my father's life, who grew up poor, the oldest son of working class people who came to Mount Airy to work in the textile mills and was the first in his family to attend college.

Arriving in Chapel Hill, Griffith encountered Edwin S. Lanier, the self-help officer for the university, who got Andy a job as a busboy in the cafeteria for eight dollars, of which five dollars was for tuition, and three dollars was to live on with free breakfast. Carl Griffith's boss, Raymond Smith Jr., claimed he helped pay for Andy's education as well. Remembering his dire financial straits at Carolina, Griffith in 1972 started a scholarship of 25 thousand dollars for sophomores, juniors, or seniors majoring in drama or music.

He wrote, in his first letter home to his parents, that boys were singing under a tree outside his dorm room, but "I didn't have the courage to go join them." One funny story from his time of living in Room 33 in the Steele Dormitory was that Griffith slept so soundly that an alarm clock would not wake him up. He hung a rope tied to his ankle out the window, and friends would tug on it as they passed early in the morning to wake him until he came to the window to let them know he was stirring. One Saturday night, a problem occurred when a group walked by after attending a party and jerked Griffith out of the window.

113

He started as a sociology major, but after failing a few classes and becoming bored with his major courses, he realized that he needed to go in another direction. He did break one record at Chapel Hill. "My counselor, a lady, called me in and said, 'Andy, very few people fail political science once, but nobody fails it twice.' I guess that was the only record I ever broke at Chapel Hill." There were not fake classes for students at UNC-Chapel Hill when Griffith attended, as there were fifty years later.

Andy went to the bishop of the Southern Province of the Moravian Church to get permission to specialize in music. He returned to Chapel Hill, changed his major to music, and started playing slide trombone in the band. He later switched to E-flat bass sousaphone. He sang in the Glee Club and started thinking about acting in the Drama Department's Carolina Playmakers.

During this time, his youthful back injury began to bother him, resulting in a trip to Duke Medical Center, where they discovered his back was out of alignment. The diagnosis placed him in a brace that cost thirty dollars. Griffith found a state program for indigent students with physical disabilities for which he qualified, which paid his tuition. Acting as a dorm manager paid for his room costs. He even collected laundry for two dollars a week.

With his medical and financial problems solved, he focused on his music and his acting. He was performing the role of Don Alhambra del Bolero in Gilbert and Sullivan's *The Gondoliers*. He would act in every musical produced while he was a Chapel Hill student, including Sir Joseph Porter's lead role in *HMS Pinafore*.

Paul Young of the choral department gave Griffith free voice lessons for working as the music librarian, which involved taking care of the Glee Club's music books. This relationship lasted for five years. Griffith became president of the Glee Club.

During the summer of 1946, Andy worked with his father, Carl, for forty dollars a week. Often hitchhiking, Griffith returned

114

to Mount Airy to perform in the auditorium that today bears his name as part of the Mount Airy Operetta Club performing such roles, such as a judge in *Trial by Jury* and Kezal in *The Bartered Bride* on November 11, 1946. This was his last public appearance in Mount Airy for over a decade.

Griffith described this time of his life as Charles Dickens did in opening *A Tale of Two Cities* as a "wonderful time and a horrible time." He took acting classes from Foster Fitz-Simmons, where Andy developed his "aw shucks farm boy" act.

During this time, Griffith's most significant opportunity was with *The Lost Colony* in Manteo, North Carolina, on Roanoke Island in 1947. The production told the story of the first attempt to start an English colony in North America. The attempt failed, and what happened to the missing colonists is still unknown. For the next seven summers, Griffith and his fellow actors lived in a deserted Navy airbase built during World War II and rode a bus to play. He started in supporting roles for two years, and for the last five years, he was Sir Walter Raleigh. Before this, Andy had never seen the ocean before, and he was so taken with the area along the Outer Banks that he made it his permanent home for the rest of his life.

Another opportunity presented itself to Griffith, and that was to perform standup routines in comedy clubs along the Outer Banks and Chapel Hill. He began with "The Preacher and the Bear" and started doing Shakespeare parodies, including "Hamlet."

During this time, in the fall of 1947, Andy met Barbara Bray Edwards in the Carolina Players at Chapel Hill. The daughter of J. S. Edwards, who was a school superintendent of Troy, North Carolina. Edwards was married to Dixie. Barbara was a graduate of Converse College in South Carolina with a music degree. Andy asked her to have coffee. It was love at first song. Griffith became so smitten after hearing Barbara sing that he proposed three days after meeting her.

115

The two went to Manteo to act in *The Lost Colony*, where Barbara played Elizabeth Dare. They were married on August 22, 1949, in the Little Log Chapel at Fort Raleigh. Griffith said that he was "married in a copy of an Anglican chapel by a Methodist minister to a Baptist maiden while a Roman Catholic vibraphonist played the pump organ."

Andy graduated with a bachelor's degree in music from UNC-Chapel Hill in 1949. Among his accomplishments was serving as president of the university chapter of Phi Mu Alpha Sinfonia, America's oldest fraternity for men in music.

After the summer job at *The Lost Colony* was over and graduation from UNC-Chapel Hill, Andy Griffith needed a job. Thanks to Clint Britton, the Lost Colony stage manager, he found one teaching drama and choral music in North Carolina at Goldsboro High School. Andy became famous for racing the students to the smoking area. The young couple moved to 1208 East Mulberry Street in Goldsboro to begin their married life. Barbara served as the musical director for two churches in the town.

After his first year, Griffith began to recruit students from his class. He soon realized he was not the greatest teacher. "I knew my subject, but I couldn't seem to pass on my knowledge. There were some gifted kids in my classes, and I felt they were entitled to the best possible instruction. Well, I didn't feel I was the best possible instructor…I couldn't handle the kids. I wasn't a good teacher.

I was happy as a child. I was happy as a teenager. I was happy as a young adult. I never had capital, but I was never unhappy because of that. When I discovered I could entertain, I worked hard at it. It's the only thing I do well. I can't be a company director. I can't be an accountant. I can't make furniture, but I can entertain."

Next came a futile attempt with the Paper Mill Playhouse in Milburn, New Jersey, in 1952. Katherine Warren of Goldsboro was giving the young Griffiths singing lessons. A friend of Warren offered the Griffiths a ride to New Jersey. The couple stayed a week in the Statler Hotel, watched the other performers, and "got scared to death by the city." Barbara sang "In the Still of the Night," and Andy sang "Dancing in the Dark."

"Someone standing around there told me my voice was overly brilliant, almost unpleasantly so. I didn't mind so much. In my own heart, I believed it. So, I decided to quit singing and start telling jokes."

Andy focused on his comedy. He got a job doing his standup routine between acts at the Raleigh Little Theater thanks to its director Ainslie Pryor. Griffith later said, "I always had a mental block about school. I was always afraid I wouldn't measure up...I'm still trying to measure up. I'm still trying to prove something to that man who said I couldn't sing. I believed him. I knew now I would never be a singer. There is a moment when the truth comes to you, and you wonder what you are going to do next."

"The Deacon Andy Griffith" continued performing with "The Preacher and the Bear," a hymn In the Pines and others. Barbara convinced him to play the Rotary Club Circuit with her, and they began an act together singing, dancing, guitar playing, and monologues with pianist Larry Stith joining them for fifteen dollars. They charged seventy-five dollars plus mileage for their unique entertainment.

They took money from Andy's teacher retirement fund and obtained loans from Mount Airy friends Jim Yokley and Robert Smith of one thousand dollars to start their venture. Yokley owned the mill, where Carl Griffith worked. Griffith described Smith as a "fine Christian man." Andy said in 2002 that Yokley and Smith's kindness fifty years earlier led him to his career as an entertainer. "I cannot be more thankful," he said.

The Griffiths moved back to Chapel Hill and worked up a promotional brochure, including photos. Griffith describes it as a "time of discovery." Their first job was at the Asheboro Rotary Club in October 1952. Program Chairman W. A. "Red" Underwood invited them, because he knew Barbara, to their annual reception and dinner for new teachers in the Asheboro schools. Underwood later said it was the "best fifty bucks that the Rotary ever spent on a program."

Barbara described those times: "We had hard times. We've gone hungry, but we were never destitute. Something always happened to help us. We didn't worry when we gave up the security of teaching and that weekly paycheck. We just knew we could make out all right. When we didn't have money, we always felt rich. Our aspirations were bigger than making money, and we had faith. We had faith in each other!"

During this time, Griffith developed his famous monologue, "What It Was, Was Football," about the "Deacon" encountering his first college football game. He claimed he came up with it driving between gigs based on a dirty joke that Vic Huggins, a Chapel Hill hardware store owner, told him. No doubt sitting in the band during college where he played tuba, observing the crowd, and the game, were also the inspiration for the comedy routine.

He performed the monologue at the Jefferson Standard Life Insurance Company convention in September 1953 in Greensboro, North Carolina. Orville Campbell recorded it for twenty dollars and released it on his Colonial Records with "Romeo and Juliet" on the B-side, splitting Griffith's profits. On November 14, 1953, the record came out the day the Tarheel football team lost to Notre Dame, 34 to 14.

Hal Cooke, a sales manager for Capitol Records, became interested in the recording and sent out Richard O. Linke from New York City. Linke eventually became Griffith's manager.

Lee Kinard, the longtime icon of WFMY in Greensboro, told a story on air, after Griffith's death. Kinard could never get Andy to come on the *Good Morning Show* for an interview, but he did encounter him at WABZ in Albemarle, North Carolina, when Griffith was as a twenty-one year old, on a public relations tour. The program director was named Gomer Ledge. It appears Andy Griffith never forgot anything or anyone he encountered as Gomer Pyle became a character on *The Andy Griffith Show* and a spin off as *Gomer Pyle, U. S. M. C.*

The success of "Football" allowed the Griffiths to pay off their debts. They moved to New York City into an apartment in Kew Gardens in Queens, at the end of 1953. Linke signed Griffith to a contract with the William Morris Agency, which resulted in an unfortunate performance on *The Ed Sullivan Show* that was a failure.

Griffith needed some seasoning, and he got it on the Southern night club circuit with shows all over the South from Florida to Texas and beyond, including performances with the future King of Rock and Roll, Elvis Presley. He saw Burl Ives, the man many of us know as the snowman on *Rudolph The Red Nosed Reindeer*. Griffith described Ives's standup routine as a "master at work." Ives said that the eyes reflect what you feel and that Andy Griffith reflected fear.

During his travels, Griffith received a copy of Mac Hyman's novel *No Time For Sergeants (NTFS)*. In 1955, the U. S. Marine Corps television broadcast of *No Time For Sergeants* appeared on the U. S. Steel Hour on ABC with Griffith in Will Stockdale's role. Many believe *Gomer Pyle U. S. M. C.* came from NTFS.

A Broadway version followed when producer Maurice Evans saw Griffith's performance. Andy became the only one to move from the television version to the Broadway version, which premiered on October 20, 1955.

Griffith said of playing Will Stockdale, "Will was the most Christian human imaginable. All the comedy came from that. It wasn't so much that the character was corn pone. It was that he was so honest and dedicated to doing right that it clashed constantly with the new society he was thrust into…"

While comedy was carrying Griffith's career, he knew he could do more, and that chance came when Elia Kazan offered him the role of a lifetime as Lonesome Rhodes in *A Face in the Crowd*. Andy Griffith left the Broadway stage for the big screen and believed it to be his career's best performance.

Years earlier, Bob Armstrong wrote a three-act play in which Griffith played the lead. In the stage play Cat On A Hot Tin Roof in New York City, Armstrong was directed by Elia Kazan. Armstrong recommended Griffith for the role of Lonesome Rhodes to Kazan.

Of making the movie, Griffith said, "It was three months out of my life I wouldn't swap for anything…He [Kazan] taught me how to relate everything I had ever heard or read to what I was doing at the moment." Before this, Griffith felt he was not cut out for dramatic roles, but his family disagreed. His cousin Evin Moore said, "They talk about Andy and his acting. He ain't acting! He's just being Andy Griffith like he always was. Now, if he ever starts acting, you'd see something!"

In May 1957, Andy Griffith began a publicity tour for *A Face In The Crowd*. The world was about to find out that he could act like someone other than a country bumpkin. Elia Kazan had just done *On The Waterfront* with Marlon Brando, and he got the best performances of their careers out of both Brando and Andy Griffith.

120

The publicity tour landed in places such as the Pioneer Theater in Andy's new hometown. The movie brought Griffith home to his old hometown as well. Much of this trip to Mount Airy has been portrayed negatively. I found little evidence of the negative. Andy Griffith proved that North Carolinian Thomas Wolfe was wrong. You can go home again.

I was reminded while revising this book of how great Griffith's performance was in the film when I saw Bruce Springsteen in 2019 on Turner Classic Movies introducing *A Face In The Crowd*. The Boss said, "He's incredible. It is just a roaring performance, and he simply never gave another one like it again, and I don't know why. It's a mystery to me. But, damn, he could act, and just an incredible performance in *A Face In The Crowd*. It is one of the most prescient pictures ever made, in my opinion. It couldn't be any more relevant than it is right now. It is about the creation of a demigod…Andy Griffith, you do wonder where that Andy Griffith went after that picture because he is so full-blooded and deep. He gets deep."

Andy Griffith's movies played at the Bright Leaf Drive-In and the Earle on Main Street, shown below as part of the exhibit at The Andy Griffith Museum in Mount Airy.

On his birthday in 1957, Andy Griffith attended a day in his honor in his hometown riding with his parents.

Andy Griffith's Hometown Welcome

Greetings old friends, Andy Griffith is shown atop a convertible as the parade unit formed in front of Mount Airy junior high school on South Main Street. Also shown are his father, Carl Griffith, wife Barbara, in front seat, and his mother (hidden by hat). (TIMES Photo)

Above and below, another view of Andy Griffith Day in 1957 seated with his parents, Carl and Geneva, in the back seat and first wife, Barbara, in the front seat.

Estimated 15,000 Watch Andy In Parade Here On Saturday

Contrary to rumors about the event, this newspaper claims 15,000 came out to see Mount Airy's favorite son during the parade and release of *A Face In The Crowd*.

The Grand Theater was in the Greene Financial building on Main Street in Mount Airy.

You Can Go Home Again

On his birthday in 1957, Mount Airy welcomed home a favorite son for "Andy Griffith Day" with a parade and several events. The cover of this book shows the happy Griffith family on that day. *The Mount Airy News* reported that on Saturday, June 1, 1957, fifteen thousand people came out to see Andy Griffith.

This event is often cited by locals not enamored by Mount Airy becoming Mayberry as the day that turned Andy against his hometown. Still, the written record does not back that conclusion. Years of rumors that the event was poorly advertised and poorly attended began the stories about Andy Griffith having ill feelings for his hometown. Still, this author found no evidence that Griffith ever said publicly about his return to Mount Airy in printed sources or anything.

Andy and Barbara flew into Winston-Salem's Smith Reynolds Airport at 9:20 a.m. A twenty-five vehicle motorcade left the airport at 11:00 a.m., coming up Highway 52, which is today the Andy Griffith Parkway, and arriving at 1:00 p.m. for lunch at what is today the Reeves Community Center and then followed by a parade down Main Street. *A Face in the Crowd* played at the Earle Theater at 3:30 p.m. and 8:30 p.m. Andy reportedly watched the first performance from the balcony. Griffith received a key to the city, and a Proctor Silex electric toaster from Surry Representative Joe Fowler Jr. Mount Airy was once "the toaster capital of the world."

Griffith wrote Mayor W. Frank Carter Jr. afterward, "I'm ashamed I've waited so long to thank you for the celebration you had for me in Mount Airy. I think the reason is that I just don't know how to thank you. I don't know that I have ever been so overcome by anything. I saw people that I haven't seen in years, and it's a real joy to know that Barbara and I have their concern and good wishes...For a while, I wondered why you did all that, but I realized you did it because you are proud, and that makes us proud. We will try to live a life that will continue to make you feel that way."

Eleanor Powell of *The Mount Airy News* wrote after Griffith's death, "Some of his classmates from prominent families thought they were a bit better than he and completely ignored the Surry County native until the actor made it to the Big Apple and Hollywood. After making his first movie, *A Face in the Crowd*, and starring in *No Time for Sergeants*, some of the local snobs traveled to New York for No Time For Sergeants' grand opening. It was payback time for Andy when the Granite City crowd claimed fame to the actor, requesting a favor to go backstage for autographs. Andy denied their requests. He would not see them nor autograph their programs. I just know he must have had a good feeling after they had treated him with disrespect in earlier days at school."

A visitor to the newspaper's website made this comment after the story appeared, "I know at least one delegation from Mt. Airy was received graciously by Andy Griffith backstage in New York at the Broadway theater, my Mom and Dad being part of it. According to them, it was a group of local dignitaries, including the perennial Mayor Maynard (Beamer), if I recall correctly. They were all nervous about who he would remember, but it was my Mother he singled out first after carefully studying the crowd. 'Why, Miss Graves, how have you been?' He said with a big grin to his former sixth-grade English teacher at Mount Airy public schools. She had always remembered him as a talented, personable student whose Father worked with hers in the Yard (furniture, lumber). I always thought he used her name as the telephone operator in the series, but could never be sure."

Still another comment from the website. "I saw him once, marching as a Girl Scout in his parade in Mt. Airy for the premiere of the movie *A Face in the Crowd*. He was riding on the back of an open Convertible, grinning widely while passing the marquee on

Main Street's movie theater featuring his film. Local bands were marching in his honor as a tribute to his musical interest. Celebrate the success of this Mount Airy Bear!"

The real story may never be known as there are people on both sides of the issue. There is no question that many in Mount Airy view Griffith's success with considerable pride and others who still want to denigrate his accomplishments. He left Mount Airy for New York the day after the celebration, but returned many times privately. It was forty-five years before he publicly let his presence be known in his hometown. He visited privately to see family and friends like Emmet Forrest, but he did not announce these visits for the obvious reason his privacy could not be contained.

Alma Venable, who now owns the Mayberry Motor Inn that features an Aunt Bee Room, was Geneva's beautician at the time. "I did Andy's mother's hair. She loved to talk about him. Andy was her only son. Andy was about all she had. And I know that he called her every day until he moved her out to California with him."

A few weeks after his trip home, Andy appeared on the television show *Person To Person* hosted by Edward R. Murrow. Richard Linke left his job at Capitol Records to manage Andy saying, "this guy's gonna be a big star."

During this time, Griffith decided to make his home along the North Carolina coast when he and Barbara purchased fifty-three acres in Manteo on Roanoke Island for thirty thousand dollars with a nine-room house on the property. Near where *The Lost Colony* is still performed, Griffith spoke of his need for open space and "No matter what happens, we know that's home, the place we can really be free…wherever else I got to be, but Manteo, that's home."

In 1957, Andy and Barbara adopted a little girl and named her after Barbara's mother. The following year they adopted a little boy, Andy Samuel Griffith Jr.

After more than three hundred performances on Broadway, filming began for No Time For Sergeants' film version late in 1957. The movie made nine million dollars, making it the fourth biggest movie of 1958. His proud mother, Geneva, stood across the street from the Earle theater, sipping Cokes both in and outside the Snappy Lunch. When the matinee was over, she crossed the street and signed autographs for people in the theater's lobby. "She was as proud of him as she could be."

Next, Andy filmed *Onionhead,* considered by many to be a cash in on *No Time For Sergeants*. He appeared on *The Tonight Show* and *The Steve Allen Show* and performed multiple times a week on the CBS radio network. He went back to Broadway, starring in *Destry Rides Again,* singing in a famous role by everyone from silent movie star Tom Mix, Jimmy Stewart, and Audie Murphy. Griffith received a Tony Award nomination for his work on the Broadway stage in 1960. His first was in 1956. Strange as it might be to readers. Griffith never received an award for his acting on stage, screen, or television.

The original purpose of this book was not to speak to the television show that brought so much of Mount Airy to Mayberry, as many far better books do that. In the eight years since the original edition came out, this author learned much more about *The Andy Griffith Show* and Mount Airy's many connections. Thus, I added more about the television show that continues to entertain people worldwide and brings people to Andy Griffith's hometown.

An operetta during the 1940's including several prominent Granite Citizens; caption describes event.

OPERETTA AT MT. AIRY TONIGHT AND SATURDAY

A group of 60 Mt. Airy musicians will present the Gilbert and Sullivan operetta, "Trial By Jury," tonight and Saturday night at Rockford street auditorium at Mt. Airy. Pictured, left to right, are: Andy Griffith, who takes the role of the judge; Earl Wray, usher; Mrs. O. Norris Smith, plaintiff; Glenn Robertson, defendant; and Louis Bianco, attorney. Mrs. Hugh Marritt and Mrs. Sparger Roberts will be accompanists. The operetta will be sponsored by Exchange, Lions and Kiwanis clubs.

Andy in Gilbert and Sullivan in Mount Airy.
Below, Andy's cousin Earlie Gilley's Automotive in Pilot Mountain.

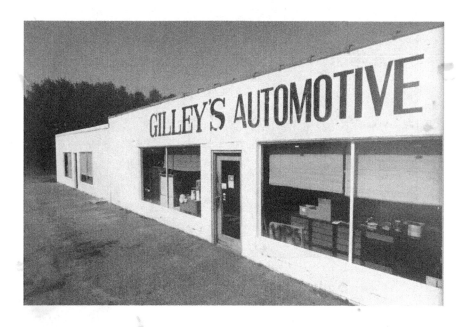

PART TWO
MAYBERRY

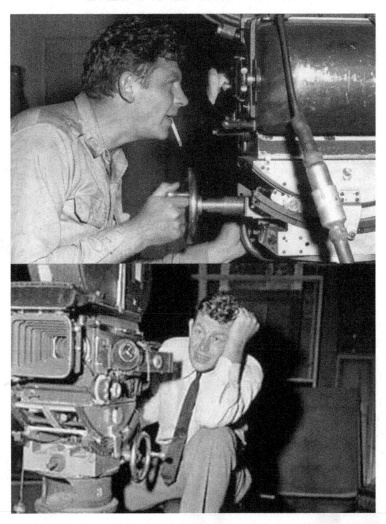

Andy Griffith behind the camera.

The Andy Griffith Show

In 1959, Griffith met with his agent Richard Linke and television producer Sheldon Leonard, who was doing *The Danny Thomas Show*. These meetings resulted in *The Andy Griffith Show*, which premiered in October 1960 after Andy's initial appearance with Danny Thomas on his show.

In 2002, Andy told the story that Leonard had the idea for a show. Griffith said he liked Leonard, but not his idea. Griffith was doing *Destry Rides Again* on Broadway in January 1959. He got a week off and went to California to shoot the pilot for T*he Andy Griffith Show* as a spinoff from *The Danny Thomas Show*.

The original idea was that Andy would be the sheriff, justice of the peace, and editor of the local newspaper, which would allow him to tell funny stories. Francis Bavier was in the pilot, where she played a woman wanting to rent the tuxedo that her husband was buried in. Ronny Howard, age five at the time, was also in the show.

Griffith described "big laughs" and sponsorship from General Foods, which got the show picked up by CBS. Don Knotts, who Griffith had worked with before, called and asked, "Don't you need a deputy?" Andy said that changed everything because he went from telling funny stories to being the straight man opposite one of the funniest men to ever appear on television.

Griffith said it best about the character of Sheriff Andy Taylor, "I guess you could say I created Andy Taylor. Andy Taylor's the best part of my mind. The best part of me." Andy's cousin Evin Moore said it best when describing the show, "Andy never left Mount Airy. He plain took it to Hollywood with him."

Sheldon Leonard wanted the show to be set somewhere in the South, but Andy wanted it to be in North Carolina. Mayberry would become a friendly town, where everybody liked one another, and all problems were solved in a half-hour. Andy started using real names of places in North Carolina like Charlotte,

Raleigh, and Siler City. He also started using real people's names Evin Moore, Emmett Forrest, Garnett Steel, J. T. Palmer, and Glen Thacker. He started using real places in and around his hometown, like Bannertown and the Snappy Lunch.

Andy Griffith recounted that in the early days of the show that producer Aaron Reuben and director Bob Sweeney came to Mount Airy to get a sense of the town "to be able to tell it right." Andy admitted that he and others pitched story ideas and worked on scripts himself, bringing Mount Airy to Mayberry.

During the Andy Griffith Show seasons, and Director Bob Sweeney would drive around North Carolina for a couple of weeks, the director could see Mayberry through Andy's viewpoint. Griffith once said about his show being based on his hometown, "There's something about Mayberry and Mayberry folk that never leaves you. No matter where life takes you, you always carry in your heart the memories of old times and old friends…"

In contrast to many of the television shows of that time that concentrated on the people out in the country like *Green Acres, Petticoat Junction,* and *The Beverly Hillbillies,* the depth of *The Andy Griffith Show* was summed by Griffith himself, "We tried to have a little message in every episode. What I would like to do, whenever I act or entertain, is to say some small truth…There's no point in doing what you don't enjoy, and if you don't do something well, you can't enjoy it."

An article in the 1961 *Mount Airy Times* provided a glimpse of Griffith's life at the time. He spent about two and one-half months a year in Manteo. His parents stayed with him, and his father Carl loved to duck hunt with the 12-gauge shotgun his son bought him. The elder Griffith retired in 1959. Carl Griffith loved to watch baseball, including trips to New York City to watch the Yankees' in the World Series.

As for the show that made their son famous, the article states the following regarding his parent's view of it all, "When

134

they first started watching his current show, it was difficult for them to grasp just what Andy was about. They understand the story better now."

In April 1966, Andy returned to Mount Airy to move his parents to California to be closer to him. He built them a house near his in the Golden State. The home contained furniture made by his father, Carl. One story from this time involved his mother, Geneva, who wanted her old bed. Andy had it shipped to her from North Carolina.

I believe that was when he encountered my father at the Hospital Pharmacy. Griffith sold his boyhood home for six thousand dollars to the Hale family on May 31. Gary York bought the house in 1998 and sold it in May 2001 for eighty-five thousand dollars. The Hampton Inn now operates it as a bed and breakfast.

During this visit in 1966, Griffith spoke to school kids at elementary, junior high, and high school, including a speech delivered from the Rockford Street School stage that began his career. He signed autographs and got a kiss from Bettsee Smith McPhail.

Carl and Andy Griffith returned to Mount Airy in 1967. "I went back there with my Dad a short while back, and I'm telling you we got lost. There's upwards of 10,000 people. You won't believe this; Main Street is one way now."

Griffith tried to leave his popular show in 1967, but CBS lured him back for one last season in 1968. The show morphed into *Mayberry RFD* with Ken Berry in the starring role. This author always believed that after Don Knotts left the show for a movie career, Andy seemed bored without his longtime partner, with whom he worked stretching back to *No Time For Sergeants*.

Griffith summed up his iconic role saying, "People ask me why it's still as popular. I always said it was because it was based on love...They allowed me to write on the show. I had to learn how to handle the script, but they allowed me to write. I did not come up with the ideas, plots, etc., but I often wrote dialogue."

Like many people, Andy Griffith looked back on life with regrets, especially his son's death. He told the television program *Entertainment Tonight*, "I think I'd do everything different." He regretted leaving *The Andy Griffith Show,* saying the show was "more my home than my home was."

In Shawsville, Virginia, the Meadowbrook Public Library made this poster for a book signing I did about *Beyond Mayberry: A Memoir of Andy Griffith and Mount Airy North Carolina.*

Many people showed up in Mayberry. Carl Griffith, Andy's father, above left in an episode. Below, *Star Trek* used the set for several episodes of the sci-fi classic.

Andy Griffith visiting Mount Airy High School's production of South Pacific in 1966 on this and next page, shown above receiving a kiss above from Bettsee Smith McPhail.

In April 1966, Andy bought his parents a new color television.

Andy Griffith Playhouse and Andy Griffith Museum.

711 Haymore Street, the boyhood home of Andy Griffith, was 197 Haymore when he lived there.

Mayberry in Mount Airy

Jim Clark of *The Andy Griffith Show* Rerun Watchers Club (TAGSRWC) said it best once, "Mount Airy's not exactly Mayberry, but it's about as close as you can get." No better authority than the man who played Barney Fife, actor Don Knotts, said in the A&E Network show *Biography* that Andy Griffith was heavily involved in the stories and the show's writing. With this information, despite the many times that Griffith himself has denied it until his visits to Mount Airy, there is no doubt that he took memories of people and places in his hometown to his television show. This chapter tells about some of them.

In 2003, Griffith talked about how the references he shared for the show were anecdotes he told the writers about growing up in Mount Airy. "I would mention names of people in Mount Airy and places in Mount Airy like Snappy Lunch, and so the people in Mount Airy got to saying it was based on Mount Airy, and that's gone on so long that I guess it just was based on Mount Airy."

The house where Andy Griffith was born at 181 South Street no longer stands. Located at Pine and South Streets' intersection, the home was near the train station on Granite Street. As previously mentioned, Griffith's boyhood home is located at 711 Haymore Street near the intersection with Rockford Street.

The Andy Griffith Playhouse operated by the Surry Arts Council was the site of Griffith's stage performance as a third-grader in the Rockford Street School. He sang, "Put on Your Old Gray Bonnet." In 2002, he performed the song again for his wife, Cindi, on the same stage.

In front of the Andy Griffith Playhouse is Andy and Opie Taylor's TV Land statue going to Myers Lake to fish as depicted in The Andy Griffith Show's opening. The statue was placed here in 2004. The dedication was one of the few public events the Griffiths attended in Mount Airy.

Charles Dowell began working at the Snappy Lunch in 1943. He bought half the business eight years later and bought the entire business in 1960, the year *The Andy Griffith Show* went on air. The restaurant is known for the "World Famous Pork Chop Sandwich." Andy Griffith ate the hot dogs in the restaurant. Episode #9, "Andy The Matchmaker," mentions the business that started in 1923 when Andy and Barney take Helen and Thelma Lou to eat.

The Mount Airy News started in 1880, is the only daily newspaper printed today. In Episode #154, "Aunt Bee's Invisible Beau," Sheriff Taylor reads a real copy of *The Mount Airy News*.

Grace Moravian Church at the corner of North Main Street and Old Springs Street was the place often sighted where Andy Griffith's career began when he started taking music lessons from Reverend Mickey. Griffith's family later joined the Grace Moravian Church, and a few years before his death, he reestablished his connections with the church. It is mentioned in Episode #240, "Barney Hosts a Summit Meeting," as a place to hold the meeting. It is one of the many buildings in Mount Airy made of granite from the North Carolina Granite Quarry.

Many real-life people became characters on *The Andy Griffith Show*, such as Sam Patterson, a real-life law enforcement officer, who could not read, write, or drive, but can be seen in many characters from Barney Fife to Ernest T. Bass. The Pile boys were based on a brother and cousin named Clarence and Homer.

Mount Airy High School's athletic teams are the Granite Bears for the granite quarry and the many black bears that still roam the area. The school holds numerous state championships in tennis, basketball, and football as of 2008. In Episode #130, "Family Visit," Sheriff Taylor wonders aloud how the Mayberry Bears are doing.

The Mount Airy Furniture Factory is mentioned in Episode #28, "Andy Forecloses," when Lester Scobey attempts to get a job at the Mayberry Furniture Factory. Carl Griffith, Andy's father, worked at the Mount Airy Chair Company, which no longer stands on Factory Street. Andy worked there as a youth and when he was home from college. The whistles from these operations were heard all over town.

Other place names on *The Andy Griffith Show* come from people and places Andy Griffith knew well. Barber Floyd Lawson came from Floyd, Virginia, and Lawsonville, North Carolina. In Patrick County, Virginia, the town of Stuart was once Taylorsville, and Andy's mother came from that part of Virginia.

Many mentions of streets in Mount Airy correspond to several episodes in *The Andy Griffith Show*. The intersection of Pine and Main Streets is the center of town. In Episode #99, Ernest T. Bass Joins the Army," Andy and Barney wait for Bass at this intersection.

Orchard Street/Road is the site of twenty-five thousand dollars stolen from a Raleigh Bank and hidden in a dry well in Episode #228, "Tape Recorder," by Eddie Blake on Ferguson's farm.

Nearby streets also contain businesses mentioned on the show. Hutchens Cleaners and Laundry on Spring Street, which is down the hill from the Andy Griffith Playhouse, opened in 1939. In Episode #50, "Jailbreak," Sheriff Taylor solves a case "thanks to the remark of the Mayberry Dry Cleaners."

Spring Street intersects Rockford Street in front of the Andy Griffith Playhouse. In Episode # 23, "Andy and Opie, Housekeepers," the stop sign on Spring Street keeps getting knocked down. Haymore and Rockford Streets' intersection, where Andy Griffith, Emmett Forrest, and others sat and told ghost stories, was mentioned in Episode #159, "Banjo Playing Deputy." Banner Street, named for the same Banner Family that Bannertown is also named for, as mentioned in Episode #5, "Opie's Charity," as a dividing line for fundraising purposes. In Episode #42, "The

Clubmen," Elm Street is the site of another broken stop sign for Barney to repair. In Episode #50, "Jail Break," Andy Taylor's address is 24 Elm Street. In Episode #44, "Sheriff Barney," Fife's address is 411 Elm Street. In Episode #13, "In Mayberry Goes Hollywood," leaders against Sheriff Taylor's protest want to cut down the "Signature Oak" to impress Hollywood producers. Willow Street in Episode #44, "Sheriff Barney," and Woods Way are the quietest streets in Mayberry.

The street most full of places referenced in *The Andy Griffith Show* is Main Street, where today, a thriving tourism economy keeps the downtown area of Mount Airy vibrant. The following are a few of the businesses either mentioned in or with connections to the show.

In Episode #45, "The Farmer Takes A Wife," Sheriff Taylor and Thelma Lou teach farmer Jeff Pruitt etiquette and get him to buy a suit from the men's clothier in Mayberry. In this show, Carl Griffith makes a cameo appearance by walking out of Carroll's Clothier of Mayberry. The men's clothier in Mount Airy is F. Rees along Main Street.

The Grand Theater was located on Main Street, where Greene Financial is located today. When I was a kid, this was the Western Auto Store. The theater held 739 people and was across the street from the Earle Theater, which still stands today and is operated by the Surry Arts Council. Episode #50, "Jail Break," shows the Grand Theater in the show's background.

Another business still on Main Street is Lamm's Drug Store. Ellie Walker (Eleanor Donahue) operated a drugstore in Episode #239, "Opie's Drugstore Job." Today, Lamm's is Walker's Soda Fountain, which is operated by David and Lara Jones. The store opened in 1925 by Lewis M. Lamm and was operated by his son, Bill Lamm, for many years. In 1945, a five thousand dollar electrical upgrade occurred in the store.

Andy Griffith went to the soda fountain at Lamm's because the school had no cafeteria. There were four soda fountains available to him. He worked one summer and delivered for Lamm's, so Andy knew all about Ellie Walker and her Uncle Fred's business.

On the opposite side of the Andy Griffith Playhouse is Moody's Funeral Home along Pine Street, once named Nelson-Moody. In Episode #107 of *Gomer Pyle U. S. M. C.*, a spinoff of *The Andy Griffith Show*, Gomer says the Marine Corps Hymn ("From the Halls of Montezuma to the shores of Tripoli") was on the back of the Nelson Funeral Parlor calendar. The Nelson-Moody building still stands just off Franklin Street on Market Street. In the 1962 episode, "Guest of Honor," Thomas A. Moody, the town honors, is a thief from a neighboring county named Sheldon Davis.

Other place names with connections to Andy include his lady friends. Ellie Walker might come from nearby Walkertown, North Carolina, or Helen Crump from Crumpler, North Carolina.

Frances Bavier (Aunt Bee) is remembered at the Mayberry Motor Inn at 501 Andy Griffith Parkway North. Owner Alma and her husband, L. P. Venable, began collecting items from Bavier's estate in 1990 in Raleigh, starting with a vanity. Several years later, Alma organized her collection into the Aunt Bee Room at the motel. Alma also had a connection to Andy Griffith as she was Andy's mother's, Geneva's hairdresser, and Alma dresses up as Aunt Bee. The room has over thirty Bavier items, including a twin bedroom suite, eyeglasses, gloves, and a dress.

Other places in Surry County are mentioned in *The Andy Griffith Show*. Among them is Pilot Mountain, known as Mount Pilot in the show. In episode #123, "Fun Girls," the two young women referred to are from Mount Pilot and want to take Andy and Barney to the Kit Kat Club. The town is home to the Miracle Salve, the Trucker's Café, and the Mayberry Bowling Team's archrivals.

Pilot Mountain is a metamorphic quartzite monadnock that rises to fourteen hundred feet above the piedmont and over twenty-four hundred feet overall within sight of the three thousand foot Blue Ridge Mountains. The name comes from the Native-American word *Jomeokee*, for "the Great Guide" or "Pilot."

Another Pilot Mountain connection is seen in Episode #186, "Goober's Replacement." Goober considers leaving Mayberry to work in Mount Pilot to go work for Earlie Gilley's garage. In real life, Earlie's wife Lorraine Beasley Gilley was Griffith's first cousin, and Earlie is mentioned in multiple episodes of the show as "Andy just loved his name."

Dobson is the county seat of Surry County. In Episode #44, "Sheriff Barney," Deputy Fife tries to find out from a sleeping Otis the location of his moonshine still, which leads through Dobson, North Carolina.

Toast, North Carolina, along Highway 89 west of Mount Airy, is mentioned in Episode #249, "A Girl for Goober," the last show, as a place to test dating services.

Other places mentioned in Mount Airy's environs include Bannertown, where in Episode #136, "Opie's Fortune," Parnell Rigsby of Bannertown RFD, puts an advertisement in the *Mayberry Gazette* for money he had lost in Mayberry. Bannertown is located along Highway 89/Business Highway 52 south and east of town along the Ararat River.

On the Old Fancy Gap Road is the Blu-Vue Motel. Episode #240, "Barney Hosts a Summit Meeting," mentions the banquet room as a possible meeting place for the "East-West Summit." The Blu-Vue was the first motel in Mount Airy, where visitors could stay and eat.

In Episode #98, "Ernest T. Bass Joins the Army," shows Andy and Barney eating at The Diner. In 1956, The Diner moved up Fancy Gap from South Main Street and Worth Street in Mount Airy to Hillsville, Virginia. "The Hillsville Diner is the oldest

operating diner in Virginia, dating back to 1925. It was built by t
Tierney Diner Company of New Rochelle, New York. It spent its
first 15 to 20 years in Mount Airy. (The black and white photo on
the next page shows it circa 1936 in Mount Airy). It was moved to
Hillsville in 1956. The interior has a counter and stool service with
no room for a booth, black and white tiling throughout, original
steel grill hoods, and 1930s back bar equipment. From a
preservation point of view, it is incredible that this fragile building
survives. It is on the National Register of Historic Places in the
Hillsville Historic District. The McPeak family have run the
restaurant since 1949. It is located at 525 Main Street in Hillsville,
near the Courthouse, the famous 1912 shootout site.

Another place mentioned in the show is Franklin. In
Episode #55, "Aunt Bee the Warden," the Gordon Boys still have
liquor in Franklin Hollow. In Episode # 59, "Three's A Crowd,"
Sheriff Taylor talks about a picnic in Franklin Woods.
Nearby places in Virginia are also mentioned in the show, such as
Fancy Gap. Episode #17, "Alcohol and Old Lace," and Episode
#155, "Arrest of the Fun Girls," both talk of the gap that is
"Fancy" because it crosses between two mountains instead of the
usual one mountain that a gap traverses.

Evin Moore, Andy's first cousin and neighbor on Haymore
Street, had several connections to the show. Evin's mother, Grace
Moore, may have been the real Aunt Bee. In Episode #166, "Off to
Hollywood," the Taylors visit Andy's cousin Evin Moore, a
Mason, in Asheville, North Carolina. Moore was a Mason in real
life. In Episode #67, "Andy's Rich Girlfriend," Sheriff Taylor talks
about taking Peggy McMillan to the Weiner Burger, which in
reality was owned by Evin Moore. The restaurant was a place
where both Andy and his mother, Geneva Nunn Griffith, worked
and was located at Rockford and Worth Streets. Geneva worked
there when Carl was sick due to his health troubles from World
War I.

149

ere were real Mount Airy people featured in Mayberry
249 episodes of *The Andy Griffith Show*, it is reported
er 150 references to the real Mount Airy. We often
....uss the places such as the Snappy Lunch or Fancy Gap, but
what about the people?

On weekdays, Mount Airy men would gather at the City
Barber Shop to talk about politics, religion, sports, and even
gardening, just like they did in Floyd's Barbershop in Mayberry.
Many people have theories about the real people in Andy Griffith's
hometown that ended up as Mayberry characters. Here are some of
those theories that I often picked up at the Squad Car Tours, where
I still swap ideas with the drivers.

One theory is that Andy Griffith is Opie. Andy Taylor is
Carl Griffith, Andy's father, who was known as a great storyteller.
One legend around Mount Airy is that Andy killed a bird with a
BB gun, not a slingshot, as Opie did in TAGS.

Floyd Pike started an electrical contracting business that
still exists today as Pike Electric. In Mayberry, Floyd became the
barber, and Pike was the last name of Mayberry's Mayors. Emmett
Forrest, Andy's boyhood friend and collector of much of the items
in the Andy Griffith Museum, worked for many years at Pike's.

Otis Brinkley and Keith Campbell, friends of Andy
Griffith, may have ended up as the name for the town drunk, Otis
Campbell.

In *Memories of Mayberry*, Author Jewell Kutzer discusses
many such people and places. One that often comes up is Sheriff
Sam Patterson, whom Andy modeled Andy Taylor on. In the
election of 1942, Patterson, a big man at 6'2", who wore a size 17
shoe, beat Sheriff H. S. Boyd. Patterson served twelve years as
sheriff when Andy Griffith came of age. In the 1986 movie, *Return
to Mayberry* mentioned that Sheriff Patterson had died, and Andy
Taylor was considering another run for office. Paul Harvey

mentions Sheriff Patterson in the *Rest of the Story* show on the radio as a model for Sheriff Andy Taylor.

Wallace Smith operated a filling station starting in the 1930s that is the model for Wally's in Mayberry. Andy's father, Carl, reportedly took his car to the station for service.

The Mayberry Trading Post near Meadows of Dan, Virginia, is thought of as the inspiration for the town's name in *The Andy Griffith Show* as written about in other parts of this book. The papers for the Mayberry Trading Post are in the Special Collections Library at the University of Virginia. Betty Lynn, aka Thelma Lou, said once that Andy talked about that place being the "Real Mayberry."

Andy's friend John Walker, pictured in another part of this book, may have been the inspiration for Walker's Soda Fountain. Today, the business that uses that name is called Lamm's Drug Store, and Andy reportedly worked there as a teenager too. These are just a few of the real people in Mount Airy that landed in Mayberry.

One of Mount Airy's places mentioned in *The Andy Griffith Show* was the Snappy Lunch, home of the "World Famous Pork Shop Sandwich."

Below, Andy Griffith used the Mount Airy newspaper as a prop on The Andy Griffith Show.

The Mount Airy News **edition that Andy was reading dates to**
May 31, 1963, and was in Season Five, Episode 27,
"Aunt Bee's Invisible Beau."

In the episode "Black Day For Mayberry," Barnie Fife was seen holding the Mount Airy phone directory.

Charles Dowell and the "World Famous Pork Chop Sandwich." Andy Griffith spoke of the Snappy Lunch in his monologue "Silhouettes," but of having a hot dog.

HOME OF THE
GRANITE
BEARS
CLASS OF 1979

Mount Airy High School's mascot is the Granite Bears.

The intersection of Main and Pine Streets in Mount Airy.

159

Andy and Opie are everywhere in Mount Airy.

Nelson Moody Funeral Home on Market Street in Mount Airy.

Pilot Mountain is real and the name of a town.

Hutchens Laundry is across from the statue of Andy and Opie.

Earlie Gilley and family in 1971.

Dobson is the county seat of Surry County.

Bannertown is located just outside Mount Airy.

Multiple murals are in the Andy Griffith Museum

The Blu-Vue on Old Fancy Gap Road north of Mount Airy.

The Diner moved from Mount Airy to Hillsville, Virginia.

The old Mount Airy City Jail, above and next two pages.

All-American Landmarks ROADSIDE ATTRACTION

OLD CITY JAIL

The Old City Jail is a re-creation of "The Courthouse" from the popular 1960s TV classic, The Andy Griffith Show, based on Andy Griffith's hometown and is reflected in the show's town of Mayberry. Once the town's real jail, the Old City Jail is surrounded by the recreations of Mayberry's favorite places to hang or enjoy.

Recognized by Hamptonville Historic Save-A-Landmark program in reference journey www.lost-architectureofmayco.com

Melvin Miles, shown above one of Squad Car Tours' drivers, headquartered at Wally's on South Main Street.

Emmett's Fix It Shop, above, and the Mayberry Courthouse, below, with cannon out front, are near Squad Car Tours.

The area around Wally's has many Mayberry memories.

175

Outside Mount Airy off Old Highway 601, there is Turner's Mountain, where in *The Andy Griffith Show,* "Checkpoint Chickie" with "Big 3 5" on the speed limit sign was on Turner's Grade.

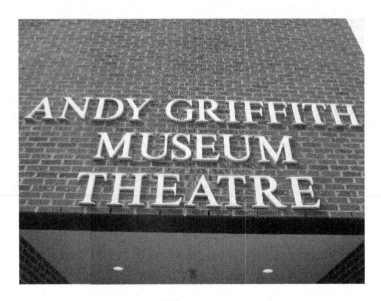

For the Briscoe Darling fans, you will remember the horse trough, shown here as a flower planter, where he dipped his hat to get some water for the radiator. Mount Airy is the North Carolina Granite Corporation's home, the largest open-faced granite quarry in the world.

Under the water tower across the street from his boyhood home, Andy Griffith flew kites from a now gone rock.

The steps of the Methodist Church, which Andy Griffith and his friends rode their bikes down.

The gulley off Creed Street was the place where Griffith played "King of the Mountain" with his friends.

On Main Street, a common site is Barney Fife's image, played by Don Knotts, on *The Andy Griffith Show*, loading his one bullet into his revolver and acting as security for restaurants that bear his name or license plates on many vehicles. Security by Fife!

Every year people by the busload visit Main Street to see the side by side attractions of the Snappy Lunch, "Home of the World Famous Pork Chop Sandwich," and Floyd's City Barber Shop. One of the few real businesses mentioned on *The Andy Griffith Show* was the Snappy Lunch. The Mayberry Effect that now dominates the town began when the City Barber Shop became Floyd's City Barber Shop.

Mount Airy is a place you can live the good life, or shop there, after getting a bite, just like Sheriff Andy Taylor and Barney Fife at the Blue Bird Diner.

Andy's cousin Evin Moore owned the Weinerburger, where
Andy's mother, Geneva, also worked.

A "Ghost Sign" was recently restored in "Canteen Alley."

"Canteen Alley" includes a memorial bench for Russell Hiatt, owner of Floyd's City Barber Shop, who first got the idea to make Mount Airy, Mayberry.

"Canteen Alley" is part of an effort to revitalize downtown Mount Airy areas and is often the site of music making.

Murals and signs are spread out all over downtown Mount Airy directing visitors to the many sites to see.

The Earle was the place to see an Andy Griffith movie.

PART THREE
BEYOND MAYBERRY

Beyond Mayberry

Only three television shows went off the air while rated number one. Among them were I *Love Lucy* and *Seinfeld*. When Andy Griffith took off his badge as Andy Taylor for the last time in 1968, he had the most popular television show. It ran for 249 episodes from October 3, 1960, until April 1, 1968, spinning off shows like *Gomer Pyle, U.S.M.C.* and *Mayberry R.F.D.* Griffith told Ron Howard that he never realized when they originally made *The Andy Griffith Show* how personal it was and how closely Andy Taylor's life reflected on his own experiences.

Andy Griffith struggled to find himself for many years after TAGS ended, acting in many roles on television, the movies, and even standup routines in Las Vegas and Lake Tahoe, Nevada. He appeared in guest starring roles on everything from *The Mod Squad* to *Sonny & Cher, Hawaii Five-O,* and even *Saturday Night Live*. Several failed attempts at a new Andy Griffith Show also occurred.

He starred in television movies such as *Winter Kill* in 1974, playing Sheriff Sam McNeill and Sheriff Sam Adams the following year in *Adams of Eagle Lake*. In 1977, he played Police Chief Abel Marsh in *The Girl in the Empty Grave* and *Deadly Game*. The year 1981 brought his memorable performance as Ash Robinson in *Murder in Texas*, for which he received an Emmy nomination. Two years later, Griffith played the bad guy against the good guy, Sheriff Johnny Cash, in *Murder in Coweta County*.

Eleanor Powell of The Mount Airy News recounted a story about her schoolmate. "I remember sitting at my desk here in the office around the late 1960s when the central telephone rang, and over the intercom, the receptionist announced, 'Eleanor Greenwood, you have a call coming in from California. It's Andy Griffith.' Waiting with anticipation and all of the reporters listening, Andy, a former high school friend, said, 'Eleanor, I need your assistance. My father has passed away, and I would like you to place his obituary in *The Mount Airy News*.' I expressed condolences, and we chatted a few minutes before he said good-bye."

It was 1975 when Carl Griffith died. The loss of his father depressed Andy for a long time. That same year, the Surry County Arts Council renamed the Rockford Street School Auditorium the Andy Griffith Playhouse. The following year he received a star on the Hollywood Walk of Fame. UNC-Chapel Hill recognized Griffith as Distinguished Alumnus in 1977.

Griffith divorced his first wife, Barbara, in 1972. She remarried in 1986. Andy married Solica Cassato, a Greek American actress, described as olive skinned and dark haired in 1975. The "unlikely couple" divorced in 1981.

Griffith returned to his faith during this time, stating, "...one Christmas when I was living alone. I was very lonely, and I called up somebody...to find out if anybody might be doing The Messiah in Los Angeles." He found a church in Glendale, California, and asked if he could sing. Griffith started attending and did so for years. He attended a Methodist church in Manteo when back in North Carolina.

Two years later, he married his last wife, Cindi Knight. Like Griffith, she came to Manteo to be in *The Lost Colony,* five years before their marriage.

In 1983, Guillain-Barre Syndrome left Griffith paralyzed and recovering through seven months of physical therapy and long-term rehabilitation. Because of this, Andy started filming *Matlock* in leg braces due to the illness. The disease started as the flu but turned into "terrible searing pain that ricocheted through my entire body."

"I owe God a lot. Beating that illness and being able to work again. I absolutely love what I do. I was given a gift, and I'm a thankful man, and I try to respect and have it, work on it, help it, and know it. That's how I try to pay the Good Lord back."

He turned to friend Leonard Rosengarten, who got him to Northridge Hospital Medical Center in California. He learned to use his mind to control his pain. It took a year for him to recuperate, and he still had permanent pain in both his feet.

Griffith fell on hard times financially and emotionally. He put his California home up for sale, but got no buyers. Andy sat in the lobby of the William Morris Agency, hoping for a job. He made four television movies, including *Return to Mayberry* and the pilot for *Matlock*. The show *Matlock* ran from 1986 until 1995, giving Griffith that rare second, hit show. The last three seasons were filmed in Wilmington, North Carolina, allowing him to permanently return to North Carolina.

During this time, he starred as Colonel Ticonderoga in 1985's *Rustler's Rhapsody* with Tom Berringer. He returned to North Carolina as Victor Worheide in 1984's *Fatal Vision, a TV miniseries* about Jeffrey McDonald's murder of his wife and children at Fort Bragg.

Summing up his life during this period, Griffith said, "Each of us faces pain, no two ways about it. But I firmly believe that in every situation, no matter how difficult, God extends grace greater than the hardship and strength and peace of mind that can lead us to a place higher than where we were before."

On March 3, 1986, Griffith began filming the pilot of *Matlock*. A month later, *Return To Mayberry* aired on April 13. A month to the day, Andy lost his mother, Geneva, on May 13, 1986.

In 1992, the Academy of Television Arts inducted Griffith in their Hall of Fame. He received a Grammy Award for Best Southern Gospel, Country Gospel, or Bluegrass Gospel Album for *I Love To Tell The Story: 25 Timeless Hymns*. More music followed in 1998 with *Just As I Am: 30 Favorite Old Time Hymns*. His last recording was *The Christmas Guest: Bound for the Promised Land*, a book and CD. The Christian Music Hall of Fame also inducted Andy Griffith.

In 1996, Griffith faced the biggest tragedy of his life when his son, Sam died. "My son died of an overdose when he was thirty-six. I was not a good father to him. My daughter is doing well. She has three children of her own and is doing well. So, I have failed in many ways."

Andy Griffith nearly died of a heart attack in 2000, and had quadruple bypass surgery on May 9. On October 16, 2002, he returned to Mount Airy for the Andy Griffith Parkway's highway dedication, a ten-mile stretch of Highway 52. During that visit, he said, "I'm proud to be from Mount Airy," indicating to many that the old bitterness was ebbing as time went on for the town's most famous son.

During the visit, Andy Griffith said, "I appreciate it. This is the biggest day of my life." He visited his cousins, Lorraine and Earlie Gilley, and his ninety-one-year-old aunt, Verdi Cook, who made him a pumpkin pie. It was his first public visit to Mount Airy in forty-five years. Getting caught up in the emotion of the moment, Andy said of Carl Griffith, "He was a great father. He was a lot better man than me. I loved him, and I still miss him. He gave me my values and my sense of humor."

Two years later, in 2004, he returned to Mount Airy for the dedication of the *Andy and Opie* statue by TV Land during Mayberry Days on September 24. During these and subsequent visits, many locals who continued the dislike of Mayberry began spreading the rumor that the Griffiths were paid to Mount Airy.

During these visits, Steve Welker, the editor of The Mount Airy News, responded in 2018 to online comments stating, "The Griffiths were not paid to come here for the dedication of the Andy Griffith Parkway. Local groups and businesses picked up the tab for some of their expenses, including complimentary accommodations." Welker also defended Andy, writing, "By the time of his death in 2012, Griffith and wife Cindi had quietly donated tens of thousands of dollars to groups and projects in

Mount Airy, including generous scholarships for young people who aspired to careers in the performing and creative arts."

UNC-Chapel Hill recognized Griffith with a Lifetime Achievement Award in 2005. He donated many items to the Southern Historical Collection at his alma mater in September of that same year, and on November 5, 2005, he received the Presidential Medal of Freedom from President George W. Bush, the country's highest civilian award along with eighteen others, including Carol Burnette, Paul Harvey, Jack Nicklaus, and Frank Robinson.

For many years, Andy Griffith was active in politics and the Democratic Party supporting Governors Mike Easley and Beverly Perdue. Griffith gave his support for years, especially to Jim Hunt in his 1984 Senate Campaign against conservative Jesse Helms. Griffith even contemplated a run himself against Helms in 1990. In 2008, he supported Barack Obama and appeared in a hilarious video made by his former television son, Ron Howard, who appeared as both Opie Taylor and later as Richie Cunningham in his role in the show *Happy Days*. In 2010, Griffith's political view backfired on his hometown when he supported Obama Care, The Affordable Care Act, which destroyed many American's health care by appearing in a government made video.

Mondee Tilley of *The Mount Airy News* wrote, "The controversy was dubbed 'Mayberrygate' by media outlets after four Republican senators, including Sen. Richard Burr of Winston-Salem, objected to the commercial. The senators wrote a letter to Kathleen Sebelius, secretary of the U.S. Department of Health and Human Services, requesting that the department pull the ad and reimburse the government for any taxpayer dollars spent on the effort."

Betty Ann Collins, President of the Mount Airy Chamber of Commerce, reported receiving communications from people canceling travel plans to Mount Airy. One irate female potential visitor said, "She did not agree with him (Andy) doing a commercial like that and was disappointed in him for doing that and ended up holding Mount Airy, because we are home of Andy — holding us responsible to where she ended up canceling all of her reservations," said Collins.

Mount Airy wished Andy had practiced what he said in his comedy monologue, "A Conversation With A Mule:" "You knew politics wasn't going to help you out none, and I am just learning."

Griffith said once he would "work till I can't remember my lines anymore." Andy Griffith's last movie role came that same year in the 2009 movie, *Play The Game* starring Grandpa Joe, a widower who seeks love in a retirement home while learning from his grandson David how to become a Lothario, including a memorable sex scene with Edna played by Liz Sheridan. The film included both Ron Howard's brother, Clint, and father, Rance.

In his last scene on camera, he is fishing with his grandson, David, played by Paul Campbell. Griffith was most famous for walking to Myers Lake to fish with his fictional son Opie Taylor, and he ended his career with a fictional grandson. Griffith's character says, "Life is good."

That same year Griffith joined country music artist Brad Paisley in the latter's video for his song "Waiting on a Woman." The last scene shows Griffith sitting on the beach in a white suit. They filmed him walking off into the sunset but did not use the footage on the video. Andy is on a beach with the wind blowing in his hair. Today, he rests on his farm near the beach with the wind from the ocean blowing over him. He is home in the soil of his beloved North Carolina.

196

A familiar scene in Mount Airy sees characters from *The Andy Griffith Show* eating a pork chop sandwich in the Snappy Lunch even though Andy Griffith never tried one to the author's knowledge.

Aunt Bee (Alma Venable) with Goober (Tim Pettigrew), Otis (Kenneth Junkin), and Floyd (Allan Newsome).

Market Street has become an area known for music and art, just a block off Main Street.

The Siamese Twins exhibit at the Surry Arts Council.

Main Street has many new historical sites, including Carlos Jones Blue Ridge Park, at the Blue Ridge Hotel location shown here with the Mount Airy Museum of Regional History in the background.

Just off Main Street on Oak Street is The Whittling Wall with sculptures by Brad Spencer of many local personalities, including Donna Fargo, Flip Rees, Fred Cockerham, Tommy Jarrell, Ralph Epperson, L. H. Jones, and a statue representing the mill workers.

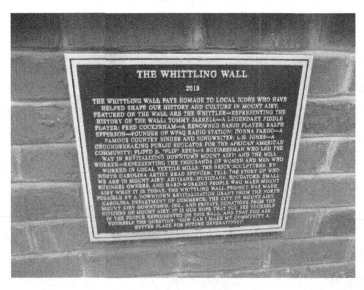

Donna Fargo, "The Happiest Girl in the Whole USA," is one of the locals depicted by The Whittling Wall.

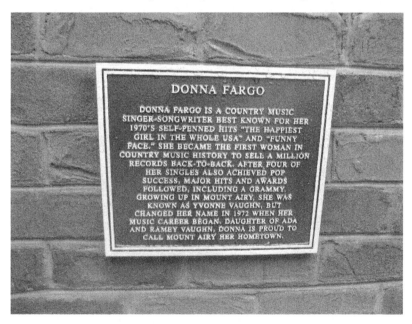

DONNA FARGO

DONNA FARGO IS A COUNTRY MUSIC SINGER-SONGWRITER BEST KNOWN FOR HER 1970'S SELF-PENNED HITS "THE HAPPIEST GIRL IN THE WHOLE USA" AND "FUNNY FACE." SHE BECAME THE FIRST WOMAN IN COUNTRY MUSIC HISTORY TO SELL A MILLION RECORDS BACK-TO-BACK. AFTER FOUR OF HER SINGLES ALSO ACHIEVED POP SUCCESS, MAJOR HITS AND AWARDS FOLLOWED, INCLUDING A GRAMMY. GROWING UP IN MOUNT AIRY, SHE WAS KNOWN AS YVONNE VAUGHN, BUT CHANGED HER NAME IN 1972 WHEN HER MUSIC CAREER BEGAN. DAUGHTER OF ADA AND RAMEY VAUGHN, DONNA IS PROUD TO CALL MOUNT AIRY HER HOMETOWN.

The Mill Worker on The Whittling Wall represents the many people, like my grandparents, who came to Mount Airy for work.

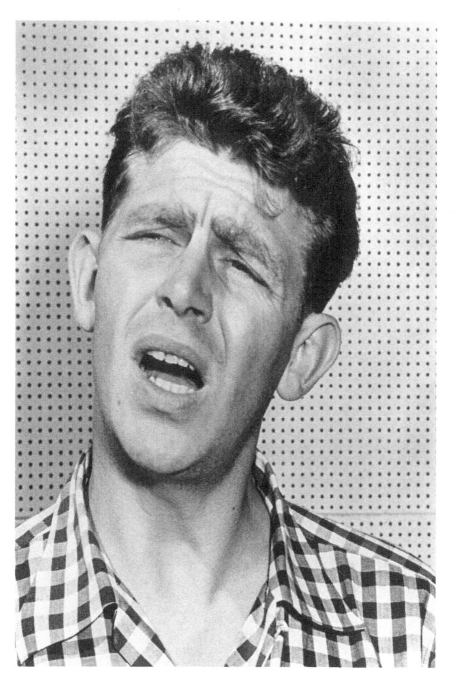

Andy Griffith

Jimmy Slate.

Mayberry on Main Street

Six Mount Airy police officers arrested Otis Campbell at 3:15 p.m. on April 21, 2011. The town drunk was arrested on Main Street, but not for public drunkenness in Mayberry. James Slate, who portrays Otis Campbell, violated the 1963 downtown sidewalk ordinance in Mount Airy, tipping off a crime wave in "Little Chicago" as Mount Airy was once known. No, Slate, aka "Otis," stated, it was for playing checkers in front of his son's store, the Mayberry Country Store, which the Slates say was once a small grocery store from which Andy Griffith delivered groceries. Slate received repeated warnings about obstructing the sidewalk before he was carted off to jail, paid a $500 bail bond, and was released. He did not have a key to the jail cell himself. Slate claimed his constitutional rights were violated.

The story of Slate, aka Otis's arrest, went viral on YouTube and multiple news outlets and online sites. Nine months passed with a continuance before a judge found Slate/Campbell guilty and charged him fifty dollars. Slate, aka Campbell, appealed to the Superior Court, stating the "ordinance is antiquated and detrimental to modern retail operations downtown."

Is Otis Campbell, a political prisoner, the victim of an overzealous police force, or is it a whole bunch of fuss about nothing? Should we start a "Free Otis" campaign and contact Amnesty International? Only in Mayberry would this be a crime, but sadly, it was in Mount Airy.

Otis vs. The Man's saga continued into July 2012 with Slate/Otis suing two police officers and the city over his arrest. The suit asks for half a million dollars, claiming loss of income and costs associated with the arrest. In the spring of 2013, a judge dismissed the case when the district attorney agreed to drop charges if Slate dropped the civil suit, thus ending the crime wave of Otis Campbell.

In the 1980s, barber Russell Hiatt, owner of the City Barber Shop, decided to promote his business as Floyd's City Barbershop, taking the name from *The Andy Griffith Show,* and a cottage industry was born in Mount Airy, one that would keep the downtown area vibrant for decades to come.

Russell was friends with my father. Like many kids growing up, I got my haircut in the same chairs that tourists now flock to sit in and get their pictures made. My grandfather, Erie Perry, came from Tennessee to North Carolina to work in the textile mills in the 1940s, and by the 1960s, he enjoyed taking his oldest grandchild up to Main Street from the West Pine Street apartment he shared with my grandmother, Idell Bates Perry. Often these trips included a trip next door to the Snappy Lunch not for a pork chop sandwich, but a ground steak sandwich or for Andy Griffith's favorite, a hot dog.

Many people have made Mount Airy home because of Mayberry, and many businesses have sprung up accordingly. Jerry Caudle started at Specialty Gifts before opening Bear Creek Fudge in the old Wolfe's Drug Store building.

Julie Marion Brinkley of Mayberry Consignments said it best in a recent issue of *Our State.* "Every small town in America would kill for what we have. The tourists come for Mayberry, but they fall in love with Mount Airy." Customers started asking Julie for Mayberry souvenirs. Julie started selling t-shirts. Mary Katherine Anthony approached her with the Andy/Opie logo on several products. Julie bought the copyrighted logo, sold hundreds of products with it, and allowed the city to use the logo on the water tower across from Andy Griffith's Homeplace.

Tourism is big business in the Granite City. In 2010, tourism brought 95 million dollars to Surry County. Among the Mayberry related businesses in town is Squad Car Tours, where visitors can ride around in a police car similar to those driven in *The Andy Griffith Show.* Among the drivers is Melvin Miles, who drives a 1963 Ford Galaxie. Miles said of the show, "A lot of parents restrict television. *The Andy Griffith Show* is probably one of the only one of them that's fit to watch." In 2011, fifty-eight thousand people visited Mount Airy and 305 thousand since 2005.

Eleanor Powell said of Andy after his death, "A friend has come and gone, and we all have fond memories that we like to share. Some we keep to ourselves. Maybe Barney Fife said it best when talking about Sheriff Andy Taylor in Mayberry, but it applies to Andy Griffith and Mount Airy. The people in this town ain't gotta better friend than Andy."

Andy in a 1946 production of *The Bartered Bride*, above.
Below with first wife, Barbara, in *The Lost Colony*.

Below, Andy was president of the Glee Club at UNC-Chapel Hill in the 1940s.

Photo Album: A Life On Stage and Screen

Men's Glee Club

Men's Glee Club

ANDREW GRIFFITH
President

Under the direction of Paul Young the Men's Glee Club has completed another successful season. Greatly reinforced by the influx of veterans, the club had a full schedule opening with the University Day program in October. A highlight of the year was the Christmas Concert in December, a combined program with the Women's Glee Club. A tour of several cities of the state was another main event, a trip in April to women's colleges in Virginia, and the Spring concert on campus.

OFFICERS

Andrew Griffith...President
William Smith...Vice-President
Charles Stanford...Secretary
Richard Cox......................................Business Manager
Dan McFarland.................................Advertising Manager

In *The Lost Colony* and with first wife, Barbara, below.

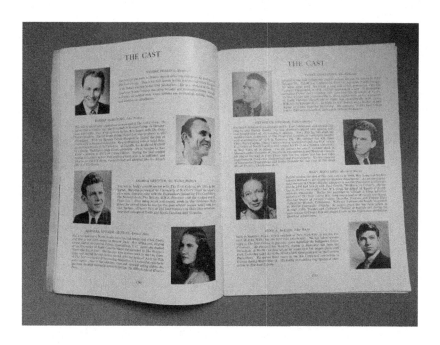

Program for *The Lost Colony* above and below members of the cast, including Andy Griffith.

211

**Andy, with first wife, Barbara, in *The Lost Colony*. He played
Sir Walter Raleigh, and she played Eleanor Dare.**

Andy is pausing for a smoke with his first wife, Barbara, in 1949 at *The Lost Colony*.

The cast of Goldmasquers entered in the Carolina Drama Festival "In-Laws" is shown above shortly before they left for Chapel Hill. Looking from left to right, they are: on the back row, David John Smith, Phyllis Banks, Harold Kadis; front row: homas Slade, Jane Elliott, Ronnie Rose, Sara Markham, K. D. Pyatt, and Gurney Collins. Standing is Mr. Andrew Grifftih.—News-Argus Photo.

Andy teaching at Goldsboro High School, shown below.

The house at 1208 East Mulberry Street, where Barbara and
Andy Griffith lived while in Goldsboro, North Carolina.

The porch at 1208 East Mulberry reminded me of the porch on the Taylor House in Mayberry. Below, the Wayne County Museum in Goldsboro tells the history of the region.

Andy in the *Mikado* in 1948 while at UNC-Chapel Hill.

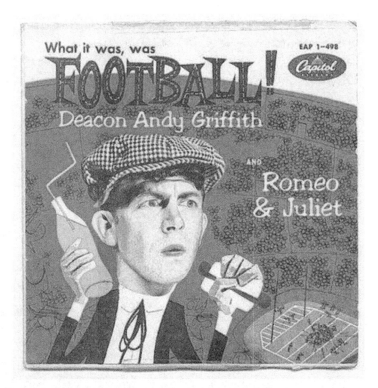

With Patricia Neal in *A Face in the Crowd*.

Andy and first wife, Barbara, during *The Andy Griffith Show*.

Andy and his first wife, Barbara, during *No Time For Sergeants.*

Andy and his first wife, Barbara, at UNC-Chapel Hill.

Andy Griffith at the Pioneer Theater in Manteo for the premiere of *A Face In The Crowd*.

Andy and Barbara at *The Lost Colony* above and below at the Pioneer Theater in Manteo.

Andy and Barbara near their home at Manteo, North Carolina, in the 1950s and 1960s.

Below, Andy and Barbara with their children.

Andy and Barbara with their children in Manteo.

Hard to believe, but there was a time that Andy Griffith was the headliner, and Elvis Presley was an opening act. Next page, yucking it up with "The King" on The *Steve Allen Show*. Below, Deacon Andy with Ed Sullivan.

Andy at home in Manteo, North Carolina.

Andy on his farm in North Carolina, and below with Barbara.

Andy and his first wife, Barbara, traveling early in his career.

Andy's first wife performed in the choir on one episode of *The Andy Griffith Show*.

Andy and his first wife, Barbara, out on the town.

Above, Andy and Barbara. Below, Barbara with Don Knotts.

Local Boy Engaged To Lost Colony Star

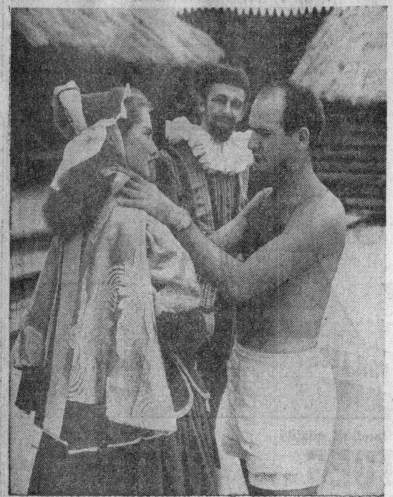

That bearded young gentleman in the background is Andy Griffith, who has the role of Sir Walter Raleigh in the presentation of "The Lost Colony" at Manteo, and the lovely young lady is his fiancee, Miss Barbara Edwards, whose make-up is being supervised by Marty Jacobs, assistant director of costumes. Miss Edwards has the part of Eleanor Dare in the drama.

Andy and Barbara in *The Lost Colony*.

Barbara is playing Eleanor Dare in *The Lost Colony*.

Andy is preparing his ammo before going hunting.

Carl and Geneva Nunn Griffith.

Left to right are Carl, Andy, Geneva, and Barbara Griffith at Manteo in the 1950s.

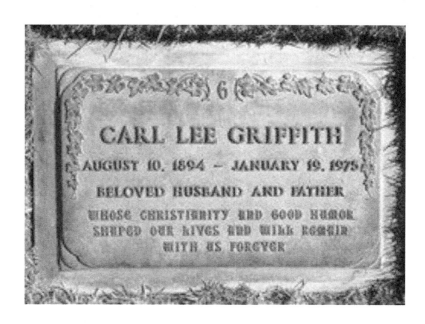

The graves of Carl and Geneva Griffith in California.

**Above, Andy's second wife, Solica Cassato.
Below with his third wife, Cindi.**

Above, Nancy Stafford starred with Andy Griffith on *Matlock,* and below is pictured with Melvin Miles on July 2012 visit to Mount Airy.

**Andy Griffith returned to television as Atlanta attorney
Benjamin Matlock from 1986 until 1995.**

Andy and his wife, Cindi, during the 2004 visit for the dedication of Andy Griffith Statue.

**Andy at the 2002 dedication of Andy Griffith Parkway
with North Carolina Governor Mike Easley, above, and below
with his third wife, Cindi.**

SPECIAL SHOWING
Andy Griffith

In the new, critically acclaimed movie ...

"WAITRESS"

Showing at the Downtown Cinema
Admission Only $3 - Rated PG-13

SPECIAL DATES & SHOW TIMES			
Friday, June 29 - 7:00 & 9:00 PM		Friday, July 6 - 7:00 & 9:00 PM	
Saturday, June 30 - 7:00 & 9:00 PM		Saturday, July 7 - 7:00 & 9:00 PM	
Sunday, July 1 - 2:00 & 7:00 PM		Sunday, July 8 - 2:00 & 7:00 PM	
Monday, July 2 - 7:00 PM		Monday, July 9 - 7:00 PM	
Wed., July 4 - 7:00 PM*		Wed., July 11 - 7:00 PM	
*Out in time for fireworks!			

**Andy received critical acclaim for his role in the movie,
Waitress starring Keri Russell.**

**Andy "Sam" Griffith Jr.'s grave at
Forest Lawn in Los Angeles.**

Above, Andy with daughter Dixie Nann Griffith in 2005 at the White House. Below, Andy with radio personality Art Hellyer in 1952.

The Andy Griffith Museum is on Carl Griffith Court at the Surry Arts Council on Rockford Street.

The set of The Andy Griffith Show, known as the "Back Forty," was once the site of the filming for *Gone With The Wind* in Culver City, California. Other outdoor scenes were filmed in Franklin Canyon near Beverly Hills. Interiors were shot at Desilu Studios in Culver City.

Andy was a strong supporter of helping mentally challenged children, as shown above in a classroom.

In Mount Airy, even granite can get artistic on Market Street.

PART FOUR RETURN TO MAYBERRY

The author still sporting his long hair from cancer
battle, with Mayor Deborah Cochran above and Donna Fargo
below, on July 4, 2012.

July 4, 2012

The day after Andy Griffith died was Donna Fargo Day in Mount Airy. The town's most famous female was coming home for several days to be the Fourth of July Parade's grand marshal. Was it a coincidence or irony that the only other person who also has a local highway named after them was in Mount Airy the day after its favorite son's death? She is a songwriter and singer of several number one hit records in the 1970s. There is no more professional or classy woman that I have ever met. When introduced at the museum on July 4th, she talked about Andy. Before her speech, she had asked me how I was feeling, as she knew I was sick. She has Multiple Sclerosis, but she would not leave until everyone that wanted to see her or get her autograph got their time with the "Happiest Girl in the Whole U.S.A."

I asked her that day if she had ever met Andy Griffith. She remembered meeting George Lindsey, aka Goober Pyle, and she thought she met Andy, but our abbreviated conversation did not lend time to much thought.

Mayor Deborah Cochran proclaimed Donna Fargo Day saying, "This lady is beautiful inside and out…Today is a great day to celebrate for all of us as Donna Fargo has once again returned to her hometown." The favorite daughter showed why she is so beloved in her hometown. "Fargo told the crowd waiting for her autograph that while the day had a somber note due to the death of Andy Griffith, she was glad to be back home. 'We were all so sorry to hear about the passing of Andy. He will be missed by all of us.' Fargo said that Griffith, through his television career, changed America. 'The show influenced our culture, and he personally showed us all how to be better people.'"

Earlier that morning, I rose early to get copies of the Mount Airy and Winston-Salem newspapers as I felt something might be of use to a historian who was writing a book about Andy Griffith and Mount Airy. The town was eerily silent, with only television crews out at the Andy Griffith Museum. There were several bouquets of flowers at Andy and Opie Taylor's statue in front of the Andy Griffith Playhouse.

I usually write about things long after they happen, but this was an opportunity to catch Mount Airy on the day it lost the most famous son. I felt the spirit of the town where I was born, and it was strong. The parade was a wonderful experience, including many squad cars like the ones driven in *The Andy Griffith Show*.

Over two hundred years ago, a group of men declared their independence from the British Empire. I thought of the old car commercial that talked of baseball, hot dogs, apple pie, and Chevrolet. I thought of how ingrained in the fabric of our nation this man from Mount Airy had become. Baseball, hot dogs, apple pie, and Andy Griffith might become a moniker for the town, as Andy mentioned his love of hot dogs during his speeches, dedicating the highway marker for him nearly a decade earlier. For anyone who ever watched *Matlock* knows that Andy often ate a hot dog on screen. This love goes back even to "What It Was, Was Football," where he famously mentions having a hot dog with a "Big Orange." He never had a pork chop sandwich at the Snappy Lunch as Charles Dowell invented that after Andy was long gone from Mount Airy. Readers will remember that Andy did make hot dogs at the Weiner Burger for his cousin Evin Moore.

At his last public appearance, Griffith said, "I'm proud to be from the great state of North Carolina. I'm proud to be from Mount Airy. I think of you often, and I won't be such a stranger from here on out."

As I thought about it, I realized that he did not owe Mount Airy anything. He had done enough. Emmett Forrest might have said it best when I saw him on television several years ago, stating Mount Airy had a four-letter tourism industry "ANDY." I am not sure Andy Griffith knew how people felt about him. I think Emmett Forrest might have summed it up best when he told his old friend, Andy Griffith, "You don't have any idea how much people love you."

Of course, they loved the character Andy Taylor, but not the real man, as few of us knew him. There was one person who did know Andy Samuel Griffith. His widow, Cindi, released the following statement on the day of his death.

"Andy was a person of incredibly strong Christian faith and was prepared for the day he would be called Home to his Lord. He is the love of my life, my constant companion, my partner, and my best friend. I cannot imagine life without Andy, but I take comfort and strength in God's Grace and in the knowledge that Andy is at peace and with God."

Griffith summed himself up this way seven years earlier, "I am just a seventy-nine year old person. I worship, and I am kind of private...I have ups and downs like everybody, but God through Jesus and prayer keeps me afloat. It fills me with joy. Even though sometimes you are not filled with joy. Sometimes you are down...I am a man like any other man. I have many failings."

Like all people, Andy Griffith was not perfect, and he was not the characters he played. He was an excellent actor and an award-winning musician just as he started at Grace Moravian Church. There is one thing that I can say about him. He brought happiness to many people all over the world and brought pride to his hometown. He is the only person from Mount Airy, North Carolina, to receive a Presidential Medal of Freedom, and as Gomer Pyle might say, "G-o-l-l-y"!

While authoring this book, I watched everything I could find on DVD in which Andy Griffith starred. In 2007, he starred in *Waitress* with Keri Russell of the TV show *Felicity* and Nathan Fillion, aka Richard Castle from the ABC Show *Castle*. Griffith played a grumpy restaurant owner who lived to eat Jenna's pies made by Russell's character. In one memorable scene, he said that if everyone could taste this pie, it could change the world.

Likewise, Andy Griffith changed the world and became as ingrained in the American psyche as apple pie.

On July 4, 2012, I left the "Happiest Girl in the Whole U.S.A." and wandered up to the Andy Griffith Playhouse. I found Patricia Comire and her fourteen-year-old son Benjamin, who had driven over from Martinsville, Virginia. after hearing of Andy Griffith's death. She was known to me as "Pat Come Here" from our mutual friend Doug Stegall of Fieldale, Virginia, who changed her name Comire to Come Here. Pat and I began to talk about *The Andy Griffith Show*. Patricia is a schoolteacher and a self-proclaimed "Helen Crump in search of her Andy." She likes Ernest T. Bass, a man on the edge. Pat asked me questions about Mount Airy and Andy Griffith, to which I replied. Benjamin who impressed me and still does as a graduate of the University of Virginia these many years later. Benjamin showed me that young people watch *The Andy Griffith Show* and that the "Love" Andy often talked about does endure. People often talk about the "Mayberry Thing" dying away, but Benjamin reminded me that many in the younger generation still love *TAGS*. He knew all about it and talked and talked.

Pat commented to me later about Mayberry and *The Andy Griffith Show,* "It has made me a little sad because I look at how things are now and wish so much that Benjamin could have those sweet, simple days. Tradition and home raising seem to be a dying art. For me, tradition, respect, and raising my child to love the Lord is natural. I just see how little of that is being instilled in other children these days."

Way out on the prairie in Topeka, Kansas, my friend Deb Coalson Bisel, who grew up in Patrick County and is now a recognized Civil War historian in Kansas, told stories to the *Topeka Capital Journal* on July 3, "People kind of craved that sense of community and connection, and Mayberry represented that to people...One of the things that Andy Griffith did for me and all people from North Carolina, is sort of the same thing that James Arness did for Kansas (Arness played Marshall Matt Dillon in *Gunsmoke*). There's an instant credibility and trust because of Andy Griffith. It's because he took that character to the world, and I'm forever in his debt for that."

A week later, Nancy Stafford, who starred with Griffith on *Matlock* from 1986 until 1992, came to Mount Airy appearing at several locations, including a tour with Melvin Miles of Squad Car Tours. In an article in the *Winston-Salem Journal*, she said of Griffith, "When I walked on that set the very first day, I was absolutely terrified. But he had a quick way of putting me completely at ease, and the whole set was welcoming...Andy was an amazing, consummate professional. He expected a lot from the people around him because he gave that, and more."

The Mount Airy News commented on the town's favorite son after his passing, "Griffith also experienced his share of controversy. He was said to be, at times, cantankerous and difficult to work with. He most assuredly was able to hold a grudge, particularly against those he perceived as having wronged him or his family during his youthful days in Mount Airy. But even in those less-than-flattering parts of his life, Griffith has much to teach us. He could be difficult, but mostly because he demanded a level of excellence for which some weren't willing to work. Andy did hold grudges, but as he aged, he became soft-hearted toward many of those who had wronged him, and he showed the humility and wisdom to put aside those hard feelings and re-establish connections. Griffith also exhibited an intense loyalty to his friends throughout his life, whether from his childhood days or people he met along his climb to his profession's top. He was quietly kind, often donating to charitable causes — many times, he footed the bill for Christmas gifts for underprivileged families in the town of Manteo — and he worked hard to keep those donations private."

Griffith worked to get WIFI on Roanoke Island. He paid for the Mount Airy High School Band back home in Mount Airy to go to Mardi Gras in New Orleans.

One aspect of the life and career of Andy Griffith that his mentor Reverend Mickey would approve of is the many churches that use *The Andy Griffith Show* to illustrate Bible lessons, including the book by Joey Fann *The Way Back to Mayberry: Lessons from a Simpler Time.* The Gateway Baptist Church in Tobaccoville, North Carolina, has Bible study after watching an episode of *The Andy Griffith Show*.

Many people believe that the 'Mayberry Daze" will pass and that Mount Airy will forget about it. Maybe when all the baby boomers like me pass on, it will not be as popular. Others believe that the simple life and ideas of living in the small southern town will go on, and that is a good legacy to have, and one Mount Airy should promote and use for its betterment. Anything else would be, as Gomer Pyle would say, a "Shame!, Shame!, Shame!"

Authoring this book has been strangely emotional for me. Either because I was fighting and beating cancer or just because I was romanticizing my father's hometown or maybe both. My focus on Andy Griffith allowed me to get back into the saddle of writing on my laptop. Taking pride in the town where one was born is not a terrible thing. The Right Honorable Mayor Deborah Cochran caught the right tone, I think, by saying that Andy Taylor was "America's favorite father" and Andy Griffith was "Mount Airy's favorite son."

The marker in front of the Andy Griffith Playhouse states, "Mount Airy to Manteo, a simpler time, a simpler place, a lesson, a laugh, a father and a son." This is the story of a father and a son, whether it is Andy and Opie Taylor, Carl and Andy Griffith, or myself and for my father, who is synonymous with Mount Airy for me.

Mount Airy is, like Paul Harvey said, a place where "everybody knows everybody, and everybody is worth knowing." In many ways, it is far superior to Mayberry, and it will always be just home for me.

Ken Ross of CBS said of colorizing the Christmas episode *The Andy Griffith Show*, "…what's better than giving families the opportunity to watch something that's pure, joyful, and wonderful? Who doesn't want to be in Mayberry?" Andy once said, "I would like to continue to give people some small thing to make them laugh. What I would like to do, whenever I act or entertain, is to say some small truth. No preaching just to have some small thing to say that is true." Amen, Deacon Andy Griffith, Amen!

Jimmy Slate, aka Otis Campbell, shown above, sued Mount Airy in 2011.

Patricia Comire and son, Benjamin, on July 4, 2012, and below
with 2012 edition of this book mentions them.

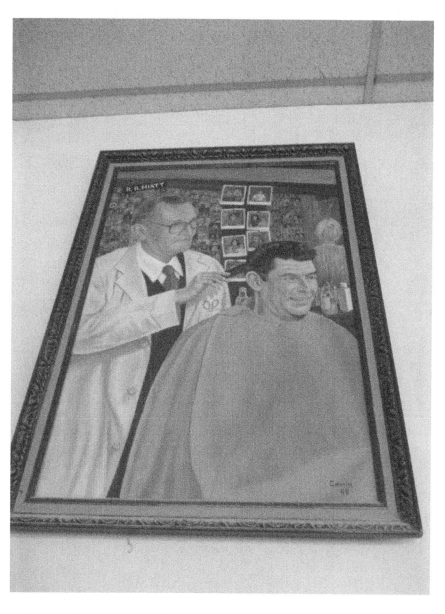

A fictional painting of Russell Hiatt cutting Andy Taylor's hair hangs in Floyd's City Barber Shop.

**Nothing like an enjoyable book about Mayberry
and a big orange.**

From Mount Airy to Manteo to Mayberry

Clergyman Henry Ward Beecher, brother of Harriet Beecher Stowe, the woman Abraham Lincoln recognized as starting the Civil War with her novel *Uncle Tom's Cabin,* once said, "Mirth is God's medicine. Everybody ought to bathe in it." Laughter is indeed the best medicine.

This book has brought me much laughter and much success in the brief time since it premiered during Mayberry Days at Mayberry on Main in Mount Airy, North Carolina, in September 2012. *Beyond Mayberry: A Memoir of Andy Griffith and Mount Airy North Carolina* was featured as part of the Virginia Festival of the Book, sponsored by the Virginia Humanities Foundation on March 20, 2013, in Charlottesville, Virginia. I was part of a panel titled "What We Write, Why We Write" at the Northside Library at 300 Albemarle Square in Charlottesville, Virginia.

"The mission of the Virginia Festival of the Book is to bring together writers and readers and to promote and celebrate books, reading, literacy, and literary culture. As the largest gathering of authors, writers, and readers in the Commonwealth, and, indeed, the Mid-Atlantic region, the Book Festival has become an integral part of the community and is presented in a unique partnership of contributors that includes the VFH, foundations, corporations, bookstores, schools, libraries, area businesses and organizations, and committed individuals. This partnership results in programs in a wide range of topics set among various venues throughout the City of Charlottesville, County of Albemarle, and the University of Virginia.

Along with the staff, every aspect of the Festival is organized and generated by Festival Committees consisting of community volunteers who generously contribute their time and energy. From a panel on how to publish a novel to a discussion on running a book club, programs range from traditional author readings and book signings to a StoryFest day of children's authors and storybook characters, from a workshop on bookbinding to a discussion on freelancer's rights. All programs are open to the public; with the exception of a few ticketed events, programs are free of charge."

Others were not enamored with the book. I had one clerk at one of the many places I sell this book to tell me, "My granddaddy went to school with Andy Griffith and said he was a jerk. I watch the show, but when they had to pay Andy to come back to dedicate that highway and that statue that says a lot about how he really felt about Mount Airy."

If you grew up anywhere near Mount Airy, North Carolina, you could not escape Andy Griffith. If you grew up as a baby boomer watching television, you could not escape Andy Griffith. Most people have an opinion about him, love him, or hate him, but you cannot deny that he is part of our lives.

He is also part of our local economy. Just drive down Main Street in Mount Airy, and there is hardly an empty storefront. Contrast that with other small towns within an hour of Mount Airy that do not have the tourist draw that is "A N D Y" as Emmett Forrest, Andy's boyhood friend, liked to say.

At Christmas 2011, I was diagnosed with prostate cancer and had surgery on February 15, 2012. I had written and toyed with the idea of writing about Andy Griffith, but I did not want to write about *The Andy Griffith Show*. I wanted to write about Andy Griffith and Mount Airy, North Carolina, where we were born. I was born about a month after *TAGS* premiered on CBS just down the street from the house in which Andy grew up.

I began to explore the common experiences and the different Mount Airys we both knew. I began to watch episodes of *TAGS*. I began to watch movies Andy Griffith starred in, thanks to Netflix. I was surprised at how good a dramatic actor he was. I went to Goldsboro and found the house where he and his first wife, Barbara, lived and the high school he taught music. I found his dorm at UNC-Chapel Hill and read some of his papers in the Wilson Library. I went through huge files at the Mount Airy Museum of Regional History, and I read many interviews and articles online.

I began to write. I found my voice again. I think the reason was that the man from Mount Airy was helping me laugh so much.

If there is anything funnier in television history than the *TAGS* when Don Knotts and Jim Nabors were on it, I have never seen it. I have always thought that after Knotts left, Andy Griffith seemed bored. It turns out he was bored and eventually left for other challenges. He struggled just as I was when I started this book, but he persevered, and he left us some of the best comedy on the small screen.

I think many times that there is much envy and jealousy aimed at Andy. To wish for the "Mayberry Thing" to go away is to wish for Mount Airy's downtown to lose the economic prosperity it now enjoys. I am against that way of thinking. You might be against the silliness or the greed that it engenders, but do not forget that Andy Griffith gave many of us pure joy in the laughter and entertainment he produced over six decades from his standup comedy, to Broadway, to movies, to television, to musical recordings, the only thing he ever received awards.

This book is part biography of the man and part memoir of the town we knew as youths. If you are looking for negative stories about him, there are few here because no one would go on record, and gossip does not interest me. What I found was a man who did not suffer fools and who was serious about his craft. He never really left Mount Airy. He took it with him, shared it with the world. Andy Griffith put Mount Airy on the map. There is only one person from Mount Airy, North Carolina, to have a Presidential Medal of Freedom, and we should be proud of him.

Andy Griffith was not Andy Taylor. I think his father, Carl Griffith, was Andy Taylor. Described as "the funniest man I ever met" by Andy's first wife, Carl Griffith was the inspiration for his son. This book is also a little about my father, who grew up the son of mill workers in Mount Airy.

John Peters of *The Mount Airy News* wrote an opinion piece titled "One of my favorite authors passed his latest book to me the other day." Peters wrote, "It was none other than local historian Tom Perry, and his latest book is *Beyond Mayberry: A Memoir of Andy Griffith and Mount Airy, North Carolina.*

"His books sometimes have a bit of a folksy feel to them. Rather than reading like an academic work, or one by a writer trying to impress us with his vast literary capability, reading Perry's books gives me the feel of someone chatting with me on the street, telling me a story. I wish more writers could figure out how to do this.

A hallmark of Perry's work, at least the ones I've seen, is a healthy dose of photos. 'Beyond Mayberry' is no exception, and this may be its strongest appeal. Don't get me wrong, I enjoy reading through the chapters — I am a writer at heart more than anything else — but the pictures he includes bring his subjects to life in ways that are difficult to accomplish with words.

I'll give you a couple of examples from his more recent effort. There is a picture of Andy Griffith from his childhood days. I don't know exactly what year, but I'd guess Griffith was somewhere between the ages of 7 and 11 when that one was shot.

It could have been a school picture, or one his parents had done of their only son. Looking at that photograph, I don't see a famous actor or musician. Instead, I see a small boy, a ghost of a smile on his face — or it's an expression of longing for something his parents cannot afford to give him. Then again, he could be thinking of what he's going to do that afternoon after the photographer is done, and he's free to run off with his friends.

I've seen that sort of expression in my own kids, and looking at that photo in the light of comparing it to my own children, I can personalize some of Griffith's life — compare some of his struggles and joys to those of my kids, or my own. And with that simple photo, Perry made the entire book more alive for me, as a reader.

That's why I enjoy local writers, such as Perry. The good ones understand how to connect with their local audience, how to bring area history alive for their readers, and I think he's done that again with his latest book."

Jo Maeder wrote a piece about the book for the *Greensboro News & Record* Published 12-23-2012. Here is that conversation.

Q(uestion): You've edited or published 35 books on regional history. This is your first that's part memoir, part biography with former Mount Airy resident Andy Griffith as the subject. What were the challenges and rewards in writing this kind of a book?

A(nswer): This book had been on my mind for a long time since I found the marriage certificate of Andy's parents in the Patrick County, Virginia, courthouse. When he passed in July, I escalated my efforts. I was recovering from prostate cancer surgery, and I used the laughter of *The Andy Griffith Show* to get me going again. This book was easy to write as I grew up near Mount Airy, and like most people my age, Andy was part of my life for as long as I could remember. This book's reception has been amazing, from people telling me how they feel about it to the amazing sales it is generating.

Q: *Beyond Mayberry* is loaded with details such as Andy Griffith had a birthmark on the back of his head, his mother called "Andy's strawberry patch." He swept outbuildings for six dollars a week to buy his first trombone. You also delve into his parents' and grandparents' past. You pored over old records in libraries and courthouses. How did you keep it organized, and was there a lot you didn't use?

269

A: Most of this book was from printed sources. The Mount Airy Museum of Regional History had a huge archive of files about Andy Griffith and Mount Airy. I did visit Andy's papers at UNC-Chapel Hill and Goldsboro, where he lived and taught school after graduating college. Everything I found is in the book, with the focus being on Mount Airy.

Q: You say Andy Griffith never said for sure that Mayberry was based on Mount Airy. His cagey reply when asked was, "It sure sounds like it, doesn't it?" There's been a bit of controversy over where the "real" Mayberry is located. Could you describe it and your thoughts on the subject?

A: In Jerry Bledsoe's book about biking the Blue Ridge Parkway, he tells about visiting the Mayberry Trading Post and Addie Wood, the owner telling about Andy visiting the place as a kid. In Andy's papers at UNC-Chapel Hill, he had a photocopy of the related pages, and the paragraph I mentioned above was circled without comment. You can read into that that Andy was pleased to see that. I think his visits to Mayberry, Virginia, were a pleasant memory of his youth with his mother's family from Patrick County, where his mother, Geneva Nunn Griffith, was from, but that is just my opinion.

Q: The photographs in the book are fantastic. Is there somewhere on the internet where they, and those not used, can be viewed? Which are your favorites?

A: Most of the photos came from people who knew Andy, Mount Airy Museum of Regional History, and the Mount Airy News. I loved the cover photo of Andy with his parents in the parade in Mount Airy on his 31st birthday, which I believe was for the opening of his movie *A Face in the Crowd*.

Q: What do you think are the biggest misconceptions about Andy Griffith?

A: I think many people assume that Andy Griffith was Sheriff Andy Taylor. He was not. I came to believe that Andy

270

Taylor was Carl Griffith, Andy's father, a great storyteller, and Andy's first wife said he was "the funniest man I ever knew," and she was married to Andy Griffith. Andy Griffith was a serious actor, and he was playing a role. In real life, he was not as approachable as the character he played.

Q: Why do you think the appeal of *The Andy Griffith Show* has endured through generations?

A: I think the Andy Griffith Show was one of the funniest shows ever on television, especially when Don Knotts was on it. I think Andy took Mount Airy with him into the show, and that made it real. I think part of the appeal of the show is that it is taken from real life.

Q: You wrote this book while recovering from surgery for prostate cancer that has side effects that, though generally temporary, could throw any man into a depression. How did writing the book help you through that time?

A: I had surgery in February 2012, and when Andy Griffith died in July, I was struggling to start work again. As I said earlier, I used the laughter from the show to heal, but it was a subject that I knew, and that made it easier to write about something so close to home for myself too. Prostate cancer for men is not easy, but I had robotic surgery at Wake Forest Baptist Hospital in Winston-Salem and am now fully functional again.

Q: What were the most unexpected discoveries you made about yourself and Andy Griffith while writing or promoting *Beyond Mayberry*?

A: I think the thing about Andy that I did not realize was how much a product of his parents he became. He got his musical ability from his mother's side, which was the only thing he ever received recognition such as Grammy Awards for his albums. He got his storytelling from his father Carl and the acting." (End of interview.)

As for myself, I think I was surprised at how much pride I began to feel for being from the same place as Andy Griffith. He received a Medal of Freedom and if you look at the ceremony, you can see the joy Andy Griffith had on his face. It is the first thing in the book because I don't think we will see anyone else from Mount Airy get one of those any time soon, and I came to understand what a memorable event that was for Andy Griffith and Mount Airy.

As the year progressed, with my recovery and the incredible success of this book, I came to feel enormous pride in Andy Griffith and the town where he and I were both born. At the many events I attended while selling this book, I heard many memorable quotes. Here are a few of them. "It says something about a show that is still on fifty-three years after it premiered." At a flea market in southwest Virginia, a fellow said to me, "The best thing about getting old and getting Alzheimer's is you get to see a new episode of the TAGS every day."

From Mount Airy, North Carolina, to Westminster, South Carolina, I encountered many people who were "Tribute Artists." These people's love of the *TAGS* sends them out all over the country, impersonating characters from the show. They are some fine folks, such as Tom Rusk, who worked with the Mayberry Festival in Westminster, now defunct, and could be a great Barney Fife with his squad car. I sat in Westminster and watched David Browning do the "Mayberry Deputy" for fifteen minutes, and I laughed the entire time. Christie McLendon portrayed "Andylina" was enormously helpful throughout my first year selling this book. Kenneth Junkin, a very sober Otis, was a great help to me.

One day in early spring, I found myself in Manteo, North Carolina. On my way back from Fort Raleigh, where the first attempt of the English to colonize failed. This is the story told in *The Lost Colony*, the play Andy Griffith appeared in and introduced via video for many years. Just down the street from the historical site and outdoor theater, I found myself in front of a locked gate with a fence that screamed, "Stay Out." It was Andy Griffith's home in Manteo and his final resting place. I did not attempt to sneak in to get a photo of his grave and risk jail time, but I did pause at the entrance to marvel at the journey from Mount Airy to Manteo he took in his eighty-plus years and the journey this book about him has taken me on over the last year.

Having years to reflect on the first edition of this book and Andy Griffith's contribution to this country and, most importantly, to his hometown, I am reminded repeatedly of Andy's cousin Evin Moore, who said that Andy did not leave Mount Airy he took it with him.

July 4, 2012.

Photo Album: Mayberry Days

On the last weekend of September each year, people from all over the world descend upon Mount Airy to celebrate Mayberry Days. Tribute Artists portraying characters from the show and surviving cast members return to get into the spirit of *The Andy Griffith Show*. Family members such as the daughters of both Don Knotts and Andy Griffith join in the festivities. The highlight of the weekend is the parade on Saturday morning, which comes down Main Street with more squad cars than you will ever see in one place at one time. Following are some photos of people celebrating the pure joy that is the Mayberry effect in Mount Airy, North Carolina.

Jim Akers might be filming the parade.

People come from all over the country for Mayberry Days,
even "War Dogs" from Auburn University.

What happens in Mayberry stays in Mayberry!

Some things in Mayberry are trivial.

Tributes To Tribute Artists

Every year people come to Mount Airy to share their love of *The Andy Griffith Show* portraying characters. These people are known as Tribute Artists. Here are some of my favorites.

Kenneth Junkin, aka Otis Campbell, might be doing a television interview. "Roll Tide!"

Ted Womack, aka Mr. McBeevee, has not only portrayed multiple characters when not rooting for the East Carolina Pirates. "Argh!" H also owns a squad car with security by Fife.

While not portraying Howard Sprague on the left, Jeff Branch is a Deputy Sheriff and DARE Officer in North Carolina. He is shown here with "KB," Kevin Burke.

At Mayberry Days, Goober and Gomer might say, "Hey!"
You can even photobomb a deputy at Mayberry Days.

Bo Pierce, who is portraying Briscoe Darling, hails from Knoxville, Tennessee, has been a member of the Mayberry Chapter of The Andy Griffith Show Rerun Watchers Club for twenty years and has attended Mayberry Days since 2008. He says, "We are a family of hearty eating men and beautiful, delicate women."

They have traveled since 2007 as Barney and Thelma Lou, Tribute Artists Ronnie and Elease Felker perform at civic groups and festivals while ministering at churches through their Fearless Fife Ministries.

Ernest T. Bass, portrayed by Phil Fox, started his Mayberry characterizations in 2000, performing as the beloved Mayberry Deputy Barney Fife opening for folk singer Leon Redbone in Charlotte, NC. In 2001, while acting as Fife in Sevierville, Tennessee, he broke out into Ernest T. Bass and found his true character. After meeting Howard Morris (who did NOT like impersonators of himself) in Mt Airy, NC in 2003, Mr. Morris asked him to do his impression of Ernest T. Bass, and at the appropriate time and place, Phil did. Mr. Morris liked it and thus started a friendship until Mr. Morris died in 2005. Phil is an Actor, Writer, Director, songwriter, and entertainer who enjoys bringing good entertainment to people of all ages.

As portrayed by Keith Brown, Colonel Harvey and his elixir have been working as the Tribute Artist of Colonel Harvey since 2009 and has appeared at local and regional events. He began traveling with the Tribute Artist group headlined by David Browning. Keith has been an educator for 40 years, 21 as a Principal. He is currently an Educational Consultant and an Instructional Technology Coach. He has been married to Angela English Brown since 1980. They have two adult married children and one granddaughter!

Duke basketball fan Tiffany Brown "grew up watching TAGS reruns, alongside my father, who was born the same year the show first premiered. The show has helped instill in me a strong sense of faith, morals, and taught me many life lessons. Because of TAGS, I've gotten to know so many people whom I consider kindred spirits. Mayberry means many things to me, but most importantly, it means family."

For over thirty years, no one did it better than David Browning, The Mayberry Deputy. He even authored a book about it, *"We Have Extra Security Tonight:" My Life As The Mayberry Deputy*.

Mayberry Things To Do In Mount Airy

Start at the Visitor's Center on Main Street in Mount Airy.

Mount Airy Visitors Center
P.O. Box 913 • 200 North Main Street
Mount Airy, North Carolina 27030-0913
Phone: 800-948-0949 or 336-786-6116
www.visitmayberry.com
Email: tourism@visitmayberry.com

Andy Griffith Day

These three photographs were taken on the parade route during Andy Griffith Day in Mount Airy on June 1, 1957, with first wife Barbara in the front passenger seat next to Mayor W. Frank Carter, Jr., and driver Bill Holcomb. Andy's parents, Carl Lee and Geneva, are on either side of Andy in the back.

The parade, held on Andy's thirty-first birthday, was part of six days of festivities in Mount Airy celebrating the premiere of *A Face in the Crowd.* Andy also received a key to the city during his visit.

The Andy Griffith Museum

The museum is open Monday – Saturday from 9:00 a.m. to 5:00 p.m. and on Sunday from 1:00 p.m. to 5:00 p.m. It is closed on Thanksgiving Day and Christmas Day. Admission includes admission to five additional Surry Arts Council exhibits, including the Betty Lynn and Siamese Twins. It is located at 218.

http://www.surryarts.org/agmuseum
Phone: 336.786.1604

The jail keys from *The Andy Griffith Show*.

The Andy Griffith Show often spoke of streets in Mount Airy, including the ones Andy lived on, such as Haymore Street, just off Rockford Street, where the museum resides.

THE CITY OF MOUNT AIRY WATER TOWER IS ON THE CORNER OF ROCKFORD STREET & HAYMORE STREET...ACROSS THE STREET FROM ANDY GRIFFITH'S HOMEPLACE. THESE STREETS ARE ALSO MENTIONED IN THE LAST BLACK AND WHITE EPISODE WITH JERRY VAN DYKE. ANDY ASSIGNS JERRY THE DUTY OF SCHOOL CROSSING GUARD AT THE CORNER OF ROCKFORD AND HAYMORE STREETS.

Family and friends are the subjects of many exhibits, including Andy's cousin, Evin Moore, shown above.

The collection includes many items from the show and Andy's personal holdings from his friend, Emmett Forrest.

The original plaques from the Mayberry Courthouse are part of the museum collection.

The museum underwent a renovation in 2017 that resulted in
Smithsonian quality exhibits on display.

Exhibits include all aspects of Andy Griffith's career, including his time at *The Lost Colony*.

Floyd's City Barber Shop

   The barbershop, located at 129 N Main Street in Mount Airy, is between the Snappy Lunch and Opie's Candy Shop. It opened in 1929 and was operated for sixty-eight years by Russell Hiatt. It is now managed by his son, Bill, a retired teacher. Known for its motto "Two Chairs No Waiting," the barbershop is a must for visitors interested in *The Andy Griffith Show*. Many celebrities and regular folks have had their photo made in one of the chairs resulting in a collection of over 60,000 images. There is no charge to visit the shop. Phone: (336) 786-2346.

Snappy Lunch

In 1923, George Roberson wanted to serve snappy lunches, "Make it Snappy," to Mount Airy workers. Snappy Lunch hasn't changed much as visitors will find the same diner that Andy Griffith ate at as a young boy while growing up in Mount Airy. Snappy Lunch started with people standing at the counters. Stools were added later. The restaurant located at 125 N. Main Street in Mount Airy is famous for its pork chop sandwich, a boneless, tenderloin chop dipped in a sweet-mile batter made from butter, egg, flour, and sugar and then fried until golden crisp. Condiments include mustard, chili, and coleslaw. In an early episode of *The Andy Griffith Show*, Andy suggested to Barney that "We can go down to the Snappy Lunch and get something to eat." Andy also mentioned the Snappy Lunch in his version of the song "Silhouettes." Snappy Lunch is open Monday through Saturday for breakfast and lunch only. http://www.thesnappylunch.com/ Phone: (336) 786-4931

300

Wally's Filling Station, Mayberry Replica Courthouse, and Squad Car Tours, and the Fruit Basket.

"There are many tips of the hat to the fictional town of Mayberry. The Mayberry Courthouse, located at 625 S. Main Street, Mount Airy, is a replica of the courthouse that appeared in *The Andy Griffith Show* during the 1960s. Situated adjacent to Wally's Service Station, visitors can sit behind Andy's desk, type on the vintage typewriter, and even sit in the recreated jail cells that appeared in the show. This is a great picture-taking spot."

"Remember Sheriff Taylor's police car? The one you saw in every episode? In Mount Airy, you can tour all the sites in a Mayberry squad car. Each tour starts at Wally's Service Station, and then it will travel up and down the streets of Mount Airy, where you will learn stories about Andy Griffith and Mayberry, the history of the town, Floyds Barbershop, the TV Land statue, Snappy Lunch, the Andy Griffith Playhouse, the childhood home of Andy Griffith, and the world's largest open-face granite quarry. Please call ahead to schedule a tour, especially during the summer and fall seasons. Keep in mind that winter hours are limited – always call before visiting." https://www.facebook.com/wallysinmayberry/ info@wallysservicestation.com

Phone: 336-786-6066 or call 336-789-6743 for Squad Car Tours tamera@wallysinmayberry.com

These fun gals, Michelle Bryson, Tamera Miles Morton, and Dixie Griffith, make this squad car look good. Tamera operates the gift shop at Wally's Service Station, where the Squad Car Tours operate. Tamera coordinates wedding ceremonies at the Mayberry Courthouse and Jail.

Squad Car Tours

On the morning of October 16, 2002, Mike Cockerham got off his third shift job to find it pouring rain. He knew it was a special day in the history of Mount Airy, North Carolina, as Andy Griffith was coming home for the first time since 1957 for a public appearance. Mike drove around town looking at the crowd, parked, put on his poncho, and found himself near the stage behind City Hall, where Andy Griffith was due to appear. As Mike stood along the crowd control rail, Mount Airy's most famous son would walk by him a little later. Everyone he encountered was from out of town, and they were asking lots of questions about Andy and his hometown.

That day an idea formed in Mike's mind. He saw busloads of tourists rolling into the town made famous as Mayberry, and they needed something to do. That day Squad Car Tours was born.

Mike discovered that the local chamber of commerce was having a contest for a business plan that could result in ten thousand dollars for the winner. He consulted with Dennis Lowe at Surry Community College about his business plan for the car ride. Mike did not win the contest, but two years later, after following his business plan to a T, he won the Small Business of the Year Award from that same chamber of commerce.

Mike was the first driver, and the first car was a 1962 Ford Galaxie that he converted to look like a squad car from *The Andy Griffith Show*.

A second car, a 1964 Ford that came from Kansas, was put in service that first summer. It was already set up as a squad car. Mike asked Julie Pharr, who was working at the chamber at the time, who she would recommend as a good driver for his new car. She replied that Jim Grimes recently retired from the chamber would be an excellent choice. Before Mike got home, Jim had called and left a message about the new job. He was the second driver within the first thirty days of the business.

303

Next came Roger Sickmiller, who now lives in Tennessee, whom Mike met at Riverside Park's playground. The third car was a 1963 model that was already set up as a squad car.

The fourth car was a 1967 model Ford as Mike wanted a car for each year of *The Andy Griffith Show*. Next came a 1965 Ford Galaxie seen in movies such as *Catch Me If You Can, Bobby,* and *Zodiac.*

The sixth car was a 1961 Ford. A seventh car from 1960 is in the works at this writing.

Squad Car Tours operates out of the former service station once owned by Wallace Smith in the 1930s, where Andy Griffith's father, Carl, got his car worked on. No doubt, Andy had a "Big Orange" at the station or maybe an "RC and a Moon Pie."

Mike met a lot of good people and admits he had a lot of help. His drivers have included Wayne Barlow, Mark Brown, Allen Burton, Donnie Bunn, Lee Clifton, Randy Collins, J. C. Fields, Mike Hill, Larry Jones, Mike Jones, Melvin Miles, Bernie Phillips, D. C. Rawley, Jonathan Semones, and Steve Talley. Mike feels blessed to have created Squad Car Tours and thinks the best thing he did was joining the chamber.

Photo Album: Allen Burton

During Mayberry Days in 2019, I came across a news story on WBTV Channel 3 out of Charlotte, North Carolina, which featured Squad Car Tours driver Allen Burton. That same day, Allen and Judy let me borrow the pictures that feature Allen's mother, Ruth Coleman, and his aunt, Lena Coleman. Other people included in the photos were Kathy Palmer and John Walker, who later became a Moravian Minister. Walker might have been the inspiration for Walker's Soda Fountain in a town called Mayberry. The reason these photos are unique is that in every picture was a friend of Andy Griffith.

Allen said in the television story mentioned above, "They come here looking for Mayberry, and they find it, but when they leave, they are going to love Mount Airy." These pictures reflect some happy times for Andy Griffith and his teenage friends in Mount Airy.

Andy Griffith with Ruth Coleman and Kathy Palmer.

Andy Griffith on the far left and John Walker on the far right.

Andy Griffith and Lena Coleman.

Andy Griffith and Kathy Palmer.

Andy Griffith on the left.

Andy Griffith and Kathy Palmer.

Two young men with Andy Griffith on the far right. John
Walker on the back row on the far left with Ruth and Lena
Coleman, and Kathy Palmer. Below, Andy Griffith with Ruth
and Lena Coleman.

Andy Griffith on the left and John Walker on the right. Below, Andy Griffith on the left with Ruth Coleman and John Walker.

Andy Griffith and Ruth Coleman.

Andy Griffith on the far right with his head down.
Below, Andy Griffith, Jack Jones, Ruth and Lena Coleman,
Kathy Palmer, Jim Midkiff, and Lib Jones.

A Night With Opie

On October 23, 2014, Mayberry descended on the Greensboro Coliseum when "Opie Taylor" came home to North Carolina. Oscar winning director Ron Howard came to be interviewed by movie critic Leonard Maltin as part of Guilford College's Bryan Series.

Howard said of the role playing Opie Taylor, which he began playing at age six on *The Andy Griffith Show (TAGS)*, "Because of *The Andy Griffith Show* and the environment that was created on that show, I learned so many things…First and foremost, trying to do something good and popular was a lot of hard work. At the same time, you could have fun. This was the great energy that Andy brought to it, there was a kind of joy in the creating, but it wasn't chaos. … When it was time to do the scene, it was all business. The other thing I really learned that I have carried with me is a spirit of collaboration."

After *TAGS*, Howard went on to portray Richie Cunningham in the sitcom *Happy Days* for six years. He branched out, making his directorial debut with the 1977 comedy *Grand Theft Auto*.

Howard acted with John Wayne, Jimmy Stewart, and Lauren Bacall in Wayne's last film, *The Shootist*. He has directed actors from Bettie Davis to Tom Hanks.

His directorial break came with the 1982 comedy *Night Shift,* starring Michael Keaton and Henry Winkler. Howard received Oscars for directing and producing *A Beautiful Mind* starring Russell Crowe. His daughter, Bryce, has starred in such films as *The Help* and the *Jurassic World* movies.

After the program, many of the Tribute Artists, The Andy Griffith Rerun Watchers Club members, and Betty Lynn met with Howard backstage. Lynn said of Howard, "He connected with the audience immediately. He was so great, and was so natural. He was just so good — all I could do was tell him how wonderful he was," she said of that conversation. "And he's still such a great boy — he really is."

**Ron Howard with Leonard Maltin
at the Greensboro Coliseum.**

The House on Haymore Street

On February 7, 2015, Jennifer Gregory of Martinsville, Virginia, did a once in a lifetime thing and stayed in the house at 711 Haymore Street that Andy Griffith grew up in and that his parents lived in until 1966. Jennifer noted that almost all the pictures were hanging crooked in the house, and she straightened them.

That day, some tourists in a squad car pulled up in front of the house, got out, and approached the building even though there are signs to discourage that behavior. They peered in the big bay window, covering their eyes with hands, and saw Jennifer, who was sitting on the couch. They waved at Gregory, who waved back. That sounds exactly like what would happen in Mayberry and does in Mount Airy, North Carolina.

When Andy Griffith returned on October 16, 2002, to dedicate the Andy Griffith Parkway, he spent the night in the house for the last time. The next day he spoke of growing up in the house on Haymore Street.

"I remember that the house had black wood siding. There were three little rooms, with a bathroom on the back porch. It was cold in there in the winter. In fact, when it snowed, the snow came through the cracks...I remember sleeping on a cot and straw mattress in the kitchen next to the woodstove to stay warm. That was the only room with heat.

When I got older, I slept in the bedroom under ten quilts. I remember standing in front of the fireplace and getting warm before going to bed. That was the good life." Griffith said of his room in the back of the house. "The happiest times I spent were in my room by myself, where no one could jeer or poke fun at me...Boy, it was a good life."

Andy said his father left the spigot running one night to keep the pipes from freezing, but the drain backed up, and they woke to two inches of ice in the basin and had to hammer the ice with an axe to use the water. When the city hooked the house up to the sewer, Andy imagined the pipe that stretched to Haymore Street was a high wire and drove his mother crazy, walking it or riding it like a horse in the wild west. Carl continued to improve the home, including adding a cement block underpinning. They dug a basement and covered the pipe, making a beautiful front yard for his mother.

Andy told of construction on Rockford Street, a concrete road, but had tar in the cracks. One day in the second grade, Andy got to school with tar on his heels, but he was covered in tar. He was sent home, and after encountering his mother, he never got in the tar again.

Today, you can stay in the Andy Griffith Homeplace by contacting the Hampton Inn in Mount Airy, about a mile away on Rockford Street. "The house is a two-bedroom home with a full size bed in each bedroom. There is one bathroom, a living room, a kitchen, and a dining area. All appliances are included."

The following pages show images of the Andy Griffith Homeplace inside and outside.

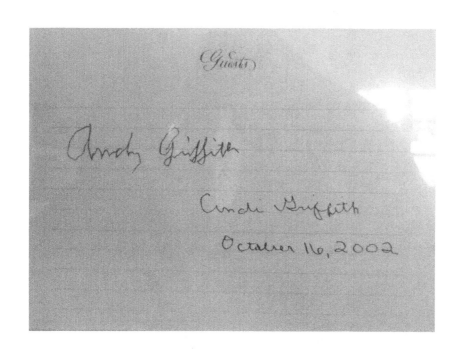

Guests

Andy Griffith

Cindi Griffith

October 116, 2002

323

Dennis Williams of Talley's Custom Frame Shop, friend of Emmett Forrest, Betty Lynn, and this author.

The Luck of Betty Lynn

For more than a dozen years at this writing, Betty Lynn, aka Thelma Lou from *The Andy Griffith Show,* has called Andy Griffith's hometown of Mount Airy her hometown as well. In 2006, Lynn returned to her home in West Los Angeles from Mayberry Days to find it burglarized, and not for the first time. She saw a billboard near her California home that said, "This ain't Mayberry!" It got her thinking that she should find somewhere else to live. "I've got to find someplace I feel safe." She found that place in Mount Airy on January 17, 2007.

The woman who would play Thelma Lou was born in Kansas City, Missouri, Elizabeth Ann Theresa Lynn, on August 29, 1926, to "Elizabeth Ann Lynn, an accomplished mezzo-soprano, who taught Betty to sing and started her in the Kansas City Conservatory of Music when she was five years old."

Her father left when she was ten months old, and her parents divorced when she was five. Her father was violent. He threatened to shoot her mother in the stomach when she was pregnant. After Betty was born, she and her mother hid in a closet as her father tossed matches under the door, trying to cause a fire. "He was nuts and it worries me that blood is in me." He tried to reconcile with her, but her mother's fear of him kept her distant from him, and she never even knew what he looked like. "I was scared to death that one day he'd walk up to me on the street."

Betty Lynn found herself on Broadway in 1940 in *Walk With Music* and *Oklahoma* in 1943. Her light soprano voice got her on USO tours during World War II. She visited hospitals singing songs to burn victims and former POWs.

Betty was discovered on the radio before Darryl F. Zanuck signed her to 20th Century Fox Studio. In 1948, she played in the movie *Sitting Pretty* with Loretta Young, Fred MacMurray, and Maureen O'Hara after getting a seven-year contract renewed in six-month intervals. Lynn said of those days, "I was a redhead with freckles and didn't have a bosom. I prayed so hard they'd keep picking me up." In *June Bride*, a role brought Betty a friendship with another actress named Bette Davis. The film also starred Robert Montgomery, father of *Bewitched* star Elizabeth Montgomery.

Two years later, she starred with Bette Davis in *Cheaper By The Dozen*. Roles in films such as *Mother Is A Freshman* (1949) and *Payment on Demand* (1950) came later. She played on television shows during the 1950s into the 1960s, such as CBS's *The Egg and I* and ABC's *Texas John Slaughter*. She played in twenty movies and on forty television shows throughout her career, including *Little House of the Prairie*, *Family Affair*, and *The Mod Squad*.

She bought a house in 1950 for her mother and grandparents to share with her. She was the breadwinner and caretaker for her family. She couldn't follow Bette Davis's advice to her, "To be a great star, you must put yourself first."

In Betty's life, the man was her grandfather, George Andrew Lynn, an engineer on the Missouri Pacific Railroad. She was engaged multiple times to the same man, an attorney, and a widower. She broke off the relationship four days before the wedding. When the bishop told her he was sorry, she replied, "I'm not!" Betty is Catholic and believed in marriage for life.

In twenty-six episodes, she played the iconic role of Thelma Lou on The Andy Griffith Show from 1961-66. Interestingly, she supplied her clothes for the show and always had to remember not to wear the same outfits. She played the girlfriend of Deputy Barnie Fife, who was played by Don Knotts. For her work she got $250 a day, which was usually $500 an episode. When Knotts left in 1966, her role as Thelma Lou was gone.

Some of her final television appearances included four episodes on Andy Griffith's show *Matlock* and the *Return to*

Mayberry movie and a final role on *Shades of L.A.* before retiring after 1991. She felt she was typecast after *The Andy Griffith Show.*

Sadly, she and Andy had a falling out during the *Matlock* shows when she wanted more than one line per script. "He wouldn't listen," she said. They did not speak to one another for twenty-two years. They last talked on June 1, 2012, about a month before Griffith's death on his birthday. He couldn't believe she moved to his hometown. She got what Andy Griffith never seemed to understand about his hometown as Lynn said, "I am surrounded by so much love."

Her mother died in 1984, and she felt like people in Los Angeles took advantage of her. By 2006, she was afraid to live in her own house and had moved to a hotel. She said it was the Blue Ridge Mountains that brought her back to Mount Airy.

When Betty Ann Lynn, then age eighty-three, moved to Mount Airy, she was the "victim of a robbery" described in the Mount Airy newspaper. Lynn lost $143 to an assailant while shopping near a Lowes Food Store. This was ironic since Betty Lynn moved to Mount Airy from Los Angeles in January 2007 to get away from the urban landscape of crime and her West Hollywood home.

She tells the story about going to the hospital for an appointment and encountering a "very proper little lady" in the waiting room. She asked the lady her name and got the response, "My name is Juanita." Remembering the Juanita from *The Andy Griffith Show,* another of Barney Fife's girlfriends, Betty responded, "You little hussy!" Both women laughed as that Juanita got the joke.

In 2016, North Carolina's Lieutenant Governor presented Betty with the Order of the Long Leaf Pine, the highest civilian honor presented by the state, at her birthday party, which took place at The Loaded Goat restaurant on Oak Street in Mount Airy and the Earle Theater on Main Street.

331

The 1965 episode of *The Andy Griffith Show* titled "The Luck of Newton Munroe," featured Don Rickles playing the episode's title character. His character is unlucky. Barnie buys Thelma Lou, a fox from Rickles's character that loses its fur in clumps, but unlike the bad luck in that episode, Betty Lynn and Mount Airy's good luck is that she now calls Andy Griffith's town her home too.

Dennis Williams of Talley's Custom Frame Shop tells the story of taking "Miss Betty" to meet Ron Howard at the Guilford College Bryan Lecture Series in Greensboro on October 23, 2014. Thirty minutes after the event, Dennis and Betty, who was in a wheelchair, were backstage when Howard appeared with security. When "Opie" saw "Thelma Lou," a big smile came over his face. "It was obvious that Howard had a lot of respect for Betty Lynn," said Williams. They had a warm conversation, and it was apparent to Williams that Howard, whom Williams described as a down to earth guy, enjoyed his time with Betty. When told it was time to leave by his entourage, Howard thanked Dennis Williams for bringing Betty Lynn.

Dennis took Betty to dinner one night and got her some Restless Soul wine from Old North State Winery in Mount Airy. She jokingly accused him of trying to take advantage of an old lady. Dennis replied he was trying to get her to tell some stories about Barney. Betty later gave Dennis an autographed photo signed, "To my second boyfriend, Barney will always be first."

Betty Lynn is at the Andy Griffith Museum signing autographs every third Friday. She charges ten dollars an autograph and has publicity shots for sale. Admission to the museum is charged to see her, but it is worth it as she is one of The Andy Griffith Show's last survivors. She once told *The Mount Airy News*, "I don't deserve as much of the love as I get." This author thinks she is wrong about that.

Betty Lynn signs autographs on the third Friday of each month at Mount Airy's Andy Griffith Museum. The following page shows the Betty Lynn exhibit near the Siamese Twins exhibit at the Surry Arts Council.

Betty, age 18, in her USO uniform.

Dennis Williams of Talley's Custom Frame Shop told me another story about Betty Lynn that is a bit of a mystery for us to ponder. While remodeling the third floor of the former Ellis Clothing Store and Duke Power office today, the frame shop, Williams was pulling down a 4x8 footboard off the wall when he realized he was standing on something that turned out to be a World War II recruiting poster. When Williams looked closer, he found two color photos of Betty Lynn in her USO uniform.

Williams saw her at Barney's Café a few days later, and afterward, she came over to the shop. When she saw the photos, tears came to her eyes, and she said, "This is impossible."

Betty told Dennis the story that she joined the USO on her eighteenth birthday, got a fitted uniform, and had a picture made. Only one color photo was made, and Lynn gave that to her mother. The others were in black and white. Her mother thought she had joined the military, but Betty explained to her mother that it was for the USO and that she would entertain the troops.

Lynn went to the Pacific Theater, where she found herself on an island full of Marines when an evacuation order came through. One of the Marines gave her a .32 caliber gun as the Japanese were attacking the other side of the island. He told her to save one bullet for herself because she did not want to be captured. Today, the gun is on display at the Surry Arts Council. Dennis donated one of the color photos to the Andy Griffith Museum, and the other hangs in the frame shop.

Author Tom Perry with Betty Lynn aka Thelma Lou from *The Andy Griffith Show* at one of her third Friday autograph sessions at the Andy Griffith Museum.

Betty Lynn with Bettie Davis.

Betty Lynn in USO during World War II.

"During WWII, starting at the age of 18, Betty Lynn performed in USO shows on the East Coast. She then signed up to perform for the USO Camp Shows overseas, which took her to Iran and Casablanca and then unexpectedly to the front lines of conflict in the China Burma India Theater. While on tour, Betty found herself in China, on the infamous Burma Road. She eventually ended up in Calcutta, where she was one of the first Americans to visit American POWs who had just been released to a Calcutta hospital after the fall of Rangoon in 1945."

Betty Lynn in the 2019 Mayberry Days parade.

Betty Lynn, aka Thelma Lou.

Darrel and Debbie Miles with Betty Lynn on her 93rd birthday.

Moving to Mayberry

Betty Lynn is not the only person who moved to Mount Airy to find Mayberry. In 1999, Darrel and Debbie Miles first came to Mount Airy, North Carolina, to take in Mayberry Days. They fell in love with the Granite City, associated with Andy Griffith, and twenty years later, they are still in Mount Airy.

After thirty-two years in manufacturing in the ice and beverage field, Darrel had reached management level after starting work with sheet metal and welding. Debbie was a stay at home mother.

Darrel and Debbie Miles grew up in southern Indiana as fans of *The Andy Griffith Show*. They are just one of the couples that came to Mount Airy because of Mayberry. Until they retired in 2018, they operated Mayberry on Main. While watching a marathon of *The Andy Griffith Show* on television, they saw Goober Pyle (George Lindsey) advertising Mount Airy, North Carolina, and saw Mount Airy mentioned on *The Oprah Winfrey* show in 1986. Vacation trips to Mount Airy from southern Indiana began over the years. "It felt like heaven," Debbie says, "Mayberry people understand each other."

Together they did something they wanted to do. In 2006, they pulled up roots in Indiana and moved to Mount Airy. Their daughters, Natalie and Samantha, along with Darrel's mother, thought they had lost their minds, but they did not care. They wanted to add a little Mayberry to Mount Airy.

The Miles opened Mayberry on Main across the street from Floyd's City Barbershop and the Snappy Lunch in today's Uncorked wine shop. After a few years, they realized that part of Main Street tended to shut down after lunch. They moved uptown to the present location of Mayberry on Main, which they felt was a better location on Main Street in Mount Airy near the Visitor's Center and is a larger space for their growing business.

343

The Miles appreciate how good Mount Airy has it due to *The Andy Griffith Show*. They were naïve about some of Mount Airy's negative Mayberry feelings, but they "live in their own little Mayberry world," and they like the positive aspects of that. They even point out that despite what people think, there were African Americans in the show's early black and white episodes and the later color episodes of the show late in the 1960s. They point out that Andy never had a family reason to come back to Mount Airy as his parents were dead, and he had no brothers or sisters. The Miles feel that "Mount Airy owes that man a whole lot. He has touched our lives in great ways."

"Mayberry people are very good people," and so is the Miles Family. Darrel and Debbie have a plethora of Mayberry items and antiques and reproduction signs. They scoff at the idea that Mayberry is dying off. Their sales got better every year they operated Mayberry on Main. Their customers were real people, who were real fans of the show that came from every state in the Union and many foreign countries. Some visitors to the store could not speak English, but they could speak the language of a shared love of *The Andy Griffith Show*. The Miles came to Mount Airy because it is the only town that Andy Griffith is from, and that is the real reason they wanted to live here. They feel it is the reason that people come to Mount Airy. They will tell you that Andy Griffith brought joy to people through his acting. They caution people not to get too far from that idea, as they worry what Mount Airy would be like without Mayberry. Sixty years after *TAGS* premiered on television, there are many worse things to be than from the "Real Mayberry."

Darrel became famous for the hot sauce that he sold on his "Wall of Flame." Many times, I saw teenage boys or unsuspecting regional television personalities like Chad Tucker of WGHP Fox 8 dare to take the challenge from Darrel, "Do you want to hurt them, or do you want to kill them?" I saw many a young man brought to his knees by the "Wall of Flame."

The Andy Griffith Show has allowed the Miles to meet many people. Nancy Stafford, who acted with Andy Griffith in *Matlock*, has also done events at Mayberry on Main. They mourn Emmett Forrest's loss, Andy's boyhood friend, who collected most of the items on display in The Andy Griffith Museum. They note the absence of David Browning, The Mayberry Deputy, at recent Mayberry Days. David was "the straw that stirred the drink" among the Tribute Artists. Others who have visited the shop include Collin Raye, Rodney Dillard (one of the Darlings from *The Andy Griffith Show*), and his wife, Beverly, James Best, Maggie Peterson, LeRoy McNees, Margaret Kerry, Jackie Joseph, Director Dick Atkins, and Producer Gary Nelson. The Miles are particularly partial to the Tribute Artists, who they call the "Spirit of Mayberry" because they give so much joy to the fans who visit Mount Airy searching for Mayberry.

They have three grandchildren, Greg, Gweneth, and Graiden, from daughter Natalie, and a grandson, Leo, from daughter Samantha.

Darrel is known for his Hawaiian shirts, sunglasses, shorts, and his ability to sweep the entrance, and the sidewalk on Main Street became a fixture to visitors and residents alike. Debbie never failed to welcome people to their store, which was famous for the great customer service, the Miles provided. They can now enjoy their grandchildren and return to what they started out being, The Andy Griffith Show fans.

Having done a plethora of book signings in the store or the alcove of Mayberry on Main, I have some great memories of my time with the Miles, especially their daughter, Samantha, bringing this starving author cookies. One of the funniest memories involved Todd Beckett from Ohio, one of the Barney Fife Tribute Artists. He set up the mannequin from the episode where Barney

345

tries to catch the shoplifters in the store. He was so good at it, or should I say so still, at it that two young ladies did not realize he was alive. When Todd moved, the young ladies let out a scream you could have heard in Siler City.

Darrel and Debbie Miles with Russell Hiatt.

Tribute Artist, Todd Becket, reenacting Barney in a scene from *The Andy Griffith Show*.

Darrel's Wall of Flame and some young victims, below.

Darrel and Debbie with grandson, Greg, and below, with David Browning, The Mayberry Deputy.

Darrel with WGHP Fox 8's David Weatherly and Chad Tucker for a Roy's Folks segment on television. Below, Chad is experiencing the "Wall of Flame."

Darrel and Debbie with grandson, Leo.

Debbie's sister, Donna Davidson Rogers, is shown with the author and Leo, has become a fixture on the Mayberry circuit. Below, Donna with the author and Melvin Miles at Squad Car Tour.

Donna corralled Goober's son, George Lindsey, Jr., at Mayberry in the Midwest in Danville, Indiana.

This author being a Darrel Miles Tribute Artist.

Darrel and Debbie Miles having Mayberry fun in Mount Airy, including a visit with Betty Lynn.

Francis Bavier as Aunt Bee on *The Andy Griffith Show*.

Aunt Bee Moves To North Carolina

In the early 1970s, Hoyt Holt of Siler City, North Carolina, was headed to the First United Methodist Church on a Sunday before returning to work at a local dry cleaning business on Monday. That day, he encountered an elderly lady and engaged her in pleasant conversation. Later that day, he realized he had come face to face with Aunt Bee of *The Andy Griffith Show* and *Mayberry R.F.D.*

Before Betty Lynn and the Miles family moved to North Carolina, Francis Bavier, who played Aunt Bee, moved to the tarheel state. She was Aunt Bee, not Aunt Bea. If you don't believe it, type the second way on social media and prepare to be savaged by The Andy Griffith Show fans.

In her book Daddy Meets Aunt Bee in Siler City, Connie Lineberry recounts her father's, Hoyt's, relationship with the most famous resident of the piedmont North Carolina town that even Andy Griffith mentioned in his famous show. Bavier requested that Holt personally handle her dry cleaning account from 1972 until he retired in 1981. It was Holt who first brought her a stray cat he noticed near his home that later blossomed into a cat family of over a dozen. He took her vegetables from his garden and got thank you notes from Aunt Bee and sometimes spelled Aunt Bea. I bet no one would have savaged her on social media. At Christmas every year, Holt got a Christmas card from Bavier that included money. When asked once if he would save the money, considering who it came from, Holt replied he would use it to pay his water bill.

In New York City, on December 14, 1902, Francis Bavier was born to older parents. When they died, her father's family raised her. She studied at Columbia University and thought of becoming a teacher until the acting bug got her. She studied drama at the American Academy of Dramatic Arts, graduating in 1925,

She moved to Broadway to perform in plays, beginning with *Black Pit* in 1935, and other plays such as *The Poor Nut*. She played a housekeeper in 1948's *Jenny Kissed Me*.

She acted in movies such as *The Day The Earth Stood Still* in 1951 and ended with Benji's last appearance in 1974. Bavier acted with Orson Wells on Broadway in 1941's *Native Son* and with Henry Fonda in *Point Of No Return*. During World War II, she did USO shows in the Pacific Theater until 1943. She acted on television in shows such as *It's A Great Life* (1954-56) and the *Eve Arden Show* (1957-58).

She was the longest running character to play on *The Andy Griffith Show* and *Mayberry RFD* playing from Henrietta Perkins on the pilot for *The Andy Griffith Show* on the *Danny Thomas Show* in 1960 to 24 episodes of *Mayberry R.F.D.* that ended in 1970. She received the Emmy Award for Outstanding Supporting Actress in 1967.

In 1972, she moved to Siler City after hearing about it from a lady on a visit to Duke University. During her life in Siler City, Bavier served as Grand Marshall of the parades. She increasingly dealt with tourists coming to see "Aunt Bee's House."

The house, built in 1952, was fortuitously for sale in 1972 when Bavier came looking. The three-story house known locally as the Doctor Earl Home became her home for the rest of her life. She painted the walls olive green, her favorite color. She had a 1966 Studebaker also painted olive green. She liked to wear a green polka dotted dress with her white gloves, pearls, and pillbox hat.

She encountered a local African-American teenager named Steve, whom she took under her wing and put to work cleaning her house and taking care of her growing brood of cats. She loved to drink hot tea and "interrogated" Steve about his life while partaking in her favorite drink. While he described her as "bossy," she practically raised the young man, allowing him to move into her home. He drove her car back and forth to other jobs, but was forbidden to drive it anywhere else. When he violated the rules, she took the keys away. When he damaged the car, she bought him one of his own. She liked to ride around central North Carolina in her Studebaker with her driver. Sadly, Steve was arrested for murder around the age of thirty.

Bavier was known for being eccentric, such as letting the leaves lay on the ground, which resulted in snakes in the yard. She liked to let nature take its course. She watched *The Andy Griffith Show*, but she did not like the color episodes like many people then and now. She sewed but only with 100 percent cotton.

Her love was her cats. She said of them, "They require little, and they accept me as I am." She brought a mother and three kittens from New York City to Siler City and the cat that Hoyt Holt gave her. Her cat family grew to as many as fifteen.

Described as difficult and "hard to please," especially during her time on *The Andy Griffith Show*, she refused to be part of the *Return To Mayberry* reunion movie in 1986. Four months before her death, she called Andy Griffith to apologize for her behavior.

Her final years revealed her to be an ardent supporter of the Christmas and Easter Seals programs. She bought lots of Girl Scout cookies from locals. Like Andy Griffith, she gave many of her papers to the Southern Historical Collection at the University of North Carolina at Chapel Hill, including photos and lots of fan mail.

Francis Bavier passed away on December 6, 1989, at her home in Siler City after returning home after a few weeks in the hospital. Her estate created a trust fund of one hundred thousand dollars for the Siler City Police Department that pays members an end of year bonus. It is believed she did this to thank them for their assistance in keeping the many tourists from violating her privacy on Elk Street. She donated to the Actors Fund of America and UNC Public Television.

Her Studebaker was bought for twenty thousand dollars at the same auction that Alma Venable purchased items that now decorate Room 109 at the Mayberry Motor Inn. The car is a 1966 Studebaker Daytona, and Bavier was a member of a club of enthusiasts for the car. It appeared in two episodes of *Mayberry R.F.D.* It still has the dents that Steve put in it.

Ted Womack, who portrays Mr. McBeevee as a Tribute Artist, found the car's DMV Registration Card, the North Carolina License plate, and Siler City plate on the car when it was purchased. Womack, who hopes to gain full ownership of the car at this writing, found sixty-three cents while cleaning the vehicle, which he would not take five hundred dollars for because it is a treasured possession that once belonged to the woman who played Aunt Bee. The car resides at the Denton Farm Park in North Carolina and is displayed as part of the annual Thresher's Reunion each summer.

If you visit Siler City, North Carolina, come in from the west on Highway 64, and stop at Oakwood Cemetery. Francis Bavier is buried on the far west side under a very upright stone that usually has jars of pickles sitting on it. They are not Aunt Bee's kerosene pickles, but that is the way people pay homage to the beloved character from *The Andy Griffith Show*. Inscribed on the stone are these words. "To live in the heart of those left behind is not to die." Aunt Bee still lives in the hearts of the fans of *The Andy Griffith Show*.

"Aunt Bee's (Frances Bavier) Studebaker. This 1966 Studebaker Daytona was Frances Bavier's last car, and 1966 was also the final year for Studebaker. Bavier played the popular Aunt Bee on The Andy Griffith Show, which ran from 1960-1968 on CBS. She would continue her part in the show's spin-off, Mayberry R.F.D., which ran on CBS from 1968-1971 (Bavier would leave the show early in 1970). Both shows fictionally took place in North Carolina.

After retiring in 1970, Bavier moved from Los Angeles to Siler City, North Carolina. She was inspired to move to North Carolina from her last two television roles. Bavier brought her Studebaker with her to North Carolina. She was a fan of Studebakers and had always driven them. She refused all suggestions to get a new car and was even a member of the Studebaker Drivers Club. Her Studebaker was used as an "extra" for street scenes on both of her shows, although The Andy Griffith Show was strictly a Ford sponsored show. It is also claimed that Bavier drove her own Studebaker on an episode of Mayberry R.F.D. Bavier last used her Studebaker in 1983."

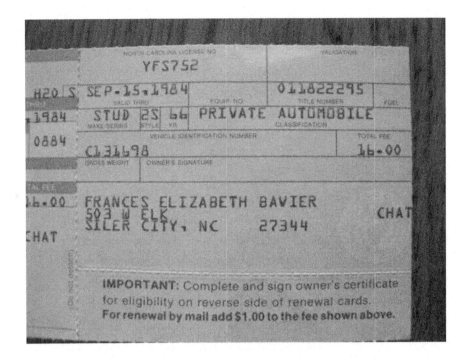

NORTH CAROLINA LICENSE NO   VALIDATION
YFS752

H2O S   SEP-15-1984   011822295
        VALID THRU   EQUIP NO   TITLE NUMBER   FUEL
1984   STUD 2S 66 PRIVATE AUTOMOBILE
        MAKE-SERIES STYLE YR   CLASSIFICATION
0884   VEHICLE IDENTIFICATION NUMBER   TOTAL FEE
        CL31698   16-00
        GROSS WEIGHT OWNER'S SIGNATURE

16-00   FRANCES ELIZABETH BAVIER
        503 W ELK   CHAT
CHAT   SILER CITY, NC   27344

IMPORTANT: Complete and sign owner's certificate
for eligibility on reverse side of renewal cards.
For renewal by mail add $1.00 to the fee shown above.

Above, Registration for Bavier's Studebaker, shown on the previous page. Below, her house in Siler City.

364

Francis Bavier and Don Knotts both won Emmys for their performances on *The Andy Griffith Show* in 1967. Below, one of the many fake images you can find on social media claiming to be a young Francis Bavier, who is Gloria DeHaven

366

Aunt Bee's Room

  Alma Venable, owner of the Mayberry Motor Inn in Mount Airy, is pictured in the Aunt Bee Room, full of items related to Frances Bavier, who portrayed Aunt Bee on *The Andy Griffith Show*. Alma began collecting the memorabilia in 1990. You can stay at the Mayberry Motor Inn as well. Information is available in the Places To Stay section of this book. Every July, the Mayberry Motor Inn is the place to watch The Andy Griffith Show under the stars near the gazebo during the annual Mayberry Meetup, including fans and Tribute Artists.

Alma Venable is portraying Aunt Bee during the Mayberry Days.

Above, Russell Hiatt's hearse slows down in front of his barbershop.

Requiem For A Barber

On Friday, May 5, 2016, a hearse slowed on Main Street in Mount Airy in front of a barbershop, Floyd's City Barber Shop. It was an act of remembrance, a requiem for a barber, and a man who did much to help bring Mayberry to Mount Airy.

His obituary stated that Russell Hiatt was born "January 28, 1924, the late Howard and Maggie Hall Hiatt son. Russell was the owner and operator of Floyd's Barber Shop on Main Street in Mount Airy for 70 years."

My grandparents lived a few blocks away down Pine Street, and many times my grandfather, Erie Perry, took me into the barbershop. At that time, there were six chairs, and sometimes you still had to wait. My father, Erie Meredith Perry, was friends with Russell Hiatt for decades, as noted earlier. I like to think that I was Russell Hiatt's friend too, as I spent many days just sitting in the barbershop listening to Russell and my father talk about their memories of Mount Airy.

I was a member of a large crowd of people who knew and liked Russell Hiatt. Everyone who came to Mount Airy searching for Mayberry made their pilgrimage to the barbershop on Main Street to get their picture made with Russell and eventually got that picture placed on the wall or in the tens of thousands of photos archived in the basement of the shop.

The barbershop opened in 1929, and Russell started cutting hair there in 1946. Three years later, my father came to town, and the two began a lifetime of friendship. When I came along in 1960, I found my way into the barbershop and got my ears lowered, as they use to say about getting a haircut, when my grandparents took me in there. These visits were usually followed by a trip next door to the Snappy Lunch. It was the heyday of *The Andy Griffith Show*, and we did not realize it, but we were living the Mayberry life.

Russell Hiatt was a generous man who would visit elderly customers when they could no longer get out. He cut hair in hospitals, funeral homes and never took money for doing it. Andy Griffith got his hair cut on Franklin Street at the Palace Barber Shop too. People from all over the world, from forty-plus countries, have visited the barbershop, including Oprah Winfrey and The Incredible Hulk, Lou Ferrigno.

Jim Clark, the Head Goober of the Andy Griffith Rerun Watchers Club, said Russell was "the uncanny virtual embodiment of Floyd the Barber…His friendship to visitors and customers extended far beyond any similarity to Floyd. Russell was indeed terrific with a razor and scissors. But his even greater legacy is that he was a terrific person and friend. Russell was as good as they come."

"There was an outpouring of love for Russell on social media," said Lizzie Morrison, downtown coordinator, who had posted a flyer announcing the procession on Facebook. As of Friday afternoon, the day Russell was laid to rest, the post had reached 60,923 people, been shared 1,100 times, received 642 reactions, and many comments and condolences, Morrison said. "He was obviously loved by so many."

An appropriate musical composition for a requiem mass for Russell Hiatt might be the simple song that we all whistle, which starts *The Andy Griffith Show*. He did more to make Mount Airy into Mayberry than anyone I know.

A True Southern Gentleman

Emmett Forrest said he could hear Andy Griffith coming down the street at night whistling or singing from his voice or music lessons when they were kids. One can see that image transferred to the beginning of a television show years later of the pure joy of a boy growing up, walking either down the street or to the fishing hole whistling.

Emmett was born in Gaston County, North Carolina, near Charlotte, in 1927. He served in the U. S. Navy during World War II. Forrest worked at Floyd Pike Electric, rising to vice-president at retirement.

In May 2012, I spied Emmett Forrest talking to Cecil Fulp, the Gilmer Smith House's groundskeeper, on Main Street in Mount Airy. I was not a good friend of Emmett Forrest, but I did enjoy talking to him whether standing on the Main Street or breaking bread in Barney's next door to our mutual friend Dennis Williams at Talley's Custom Frame Shop. Forrest always liked to talk with me about the Civil War. We decided he was related to Nathan Bedford Forrest, one of two men to go from private to lieutenant general for the Confederacy in the War Between the States. Wade Hampton was the other.

Over the years, Emmett took it upon himself to collect Andy Griffith memorabilia and received many things from Andy himself. For many years, the collection was on display at the Robert Smith House, "The Blue House," owned by the Gilmer Smith House Foundation on North Main Street, and the Donna Fargo Collection. Emmett wanted it free for people to see and was reluctant until late in life to charge anyone to see his collection. Ann Vaughan operated the Gilmer Smith Foundation and, for many years, was an essential player in bringing visitors to Mount Airy.

The Mount Airy Museum of Regional History lost a fantastic opportunity to host Emmett's collection, which would

373

have funded the museum for years to come. This was due to the museum's leadership looking down on Mayberry Effect and offending Emmett Forrest personally. I know this because Emmett showed me the copies he carried in his wallet of editorials by the museum director, Barbara Summerlin when she was editor of the *Mount Airy News* that were derogatory about Andy in Mount Airy.

Emmett Forrest, another of those named in *The Andy Griffith Show* as Emmett, "The Fix It Man." The real Emmett has done his friend Andy, and his hometown, a great service in collecting and preserving this collection of memorabilia.

One of Emmett's daughters commented on the relationship between her father and Griffith. They stayed close for all their lives. Over the years, Emmett collected memorabilia, gathering it from Andy whenever he was willing to part with it. Once, while her father was visiting Andy at his home on Roanoke Island, Andy urged Emmett to follow him out to the garage to see his latest project. Andy loved to collect and restore old cars.

"When they got out to the garage, Daddy noticed the signs (Sheriff and Justice of the Peace), which hung on the outside jail doors on *The Andy Griffith Show*. Forrest said, 'Andy, where those come from?' Andy shrugged, 'Oh, I've had those ever since the old show ended.' Daddy said, 'Oh, Andy, we need those for the museum."

"On one of the special occasions, town officials sent a plane to bring Andy and his wife. The pilots were loading the plane and noticed that Andy was holding a box. 'We'll load that for you.' Andy hugged the box tightly and said, 'Oh no. This box stays with me.' He held it on the flight in his lap then asked to be driven to Emmett's house, the box still cradled in his arms. Andy came in and said, 'Emmett, I brought you something.' Daddy opened the box, and there were the signs."

As part of the Andy Griffith Museum, doors identical to Sheriff Taylor's office are prominently featured with those original signs. Griffith's uniform, also displayed, was made by the designer Nudie Cohn, who made the elaborate rhinestone suits for Hank Williams and Porter Wagoner.

"Andy wanted me to have this collection because he knew I would never sell it. He knew that it would be available for the public to see," Forrest said in an interview with *The Mount Airy News*.

One day Dennis Williams and his son, Zach, were stopped at a stoplight in Mount Airy. Zach pointed out to his dad that Emmett Forrest was in the car beside him and tried to get his attention. Dennis looked over and saw Emmett pointing to the back seat. When Williams looked, he saw Andy and Cindi Griffith waving at him.

Dennis Williams retired in 1997 and moved to Mount Airy as a single parent. He met Emmett Forrest at a Veteran's Day celebration. Williams came from a military family. His father spent twenty-six years in the Army, including time being a POW in Korea. His brothers were officers.

Dennis spent twenty-two years in the Marine Corps. He served under Colonel Oliver North, whom he is still impressed by to this day. Dennis met Presidents Reagan, George H. W. Bush, and George W. Bush. Reagan loved to ride horses at Quantico Marine Camp, and Dennis was part of the detail that rode with him many times. He was not close to President Reagan, but he found him to be sharp, and he believes the idea that Reagan had Alzheimer's while in office is not true.

Emmett Forrest said of himself and Andy growing up in Mount Airy, in Jewell Mitchell Kutzer's book *Memories of Mayberry*, "Andy and I came from the same working-class background and experienced both the challenges and the freedom that exists in a small town. We didn't have much money, so we learned to make the best of what we had. My memories of the time we spent together bring me pleasure. I'm very proud of what Andy has accomplished."

Williams and Forrest would eat lunch at Barney's Café. It was not until later he discovered that Forrest was Andy Griffith's friend. He told Williams about an elementary school picture in which everything Forrest was wearing in that picture except socks and underwear, he borrowed. To make the point about how poor he and Griffith were growing up, he said Andy also borrowed everything except his socks and shoes.

Williams disputes the idea that Andy Griffith never came to Mount Airy. Griffith was a private person who did not advertise his trips home. Williams tells the story that he got a call from Forrest one night, telling him to come over to the house. Williams roused his sleeping son, Zach, at 9:00 p.m. and went over to 1740 Inglebrook Trail in Mount Airy. When he entered the house, Williams noticed a familiar lady sitting in a chair, and he heard a familiar voice saying, "Hey, I heard you wanted to meet me." It was Andy Griffith. Williams extended his hand, and Griffith replied, "Oh no, I am a hugger." Dennis Williams found himself in the embrace of Mount Airy's most famous son. Griffith hugged Zach too. It was three hours before they left, well after midnight, and Williams says he could have listened to them all night.

Williams says he met Griffith privately three times over the years due to his friendship with Forrest. He could tell that Griffith's health was in decline and he could be cranky due to medication and age, but Williams says he felt privileged that Forrest trusted him enough to allow him access to the friendship between the two men, and he wished he had spent more time with Forrest and Griffith.

Dennis Williams's relationship with Emmett Forrest left him privy to many stories that would be unknown otherwise. Two of these involve Andy Griffith and Grace Moravian Church.

For starters, after Griffith's death in July 2012, there was no secret burial crew digging at Grace Moravian Church. Betty Woltz died a day or two before Andy Griffith, and as a Moravian, she was going to be buried at the cemetery, God's Acre. Dennis remembers seeing people stopped at the cemetery taking pictures of the freshly dug grave, probably believing they had the scoop on Andy's grave at the church that started his career with Reverend Mickey. They did not know that men and women are segregated at the cemetery, with men and women on opposite sides of the burial yard.

Sadly, Andy's burial at the church almost came to fruition. One of Williams' stories is the fiasco that was Andy joining Grace Moravian Church. In 2009, *The Mount Airy News* reported that Griffith had reestablished his relationship with Grace Moravian Church with an "affirmation of faith." The reverend, his wife, and Emmett Forrest traveled to Manteo to meet with Griffith. The newspaper article stated, "Membership in Grace Moravian Church could lead to Griffith's future interment in God's Acre, the church cemetery bordering North Main Street where graves are marked with simple flat stones in keeping with Moravian tradition." Andy Griffith's life and career had come full circle back to the church, where his love of music was nurtured and where the faith that was so important to him was reaffirmed.

Emmett Forrest told Williams about Andy Griffith made a "secret visit" to Mount Airy because he wanted to come home and be buried at God's Acre. He met with the new minister to discuss it and made it plain that it was to stay a secret.

Williams walked into Barney's Café one day and found Emmett with a "disgusted look on his face." Forrest told Williams, "The gig is up," and explained that the preacher and his wife had been telling people about what Griffith had wanted to be a private matter. Williams wondered aloud to what the pastor was thinking, as Emmett was a church member and would certainly be the first person people would approach. Williams witnessed Forrest's call to Andy Griffith to let him know. The reaction on the other end of the phone included a few choice words. Griffith expressed he was not going through a circus. Andy did not want Grace Moravian to become Graceland, with tourists descending on God's Acre upon his death.

To this day, people still whisper that they know Andy is buried at Grace Moravian, but I have it on good authority he is buried on his farm in Mateo on Roanoke Island with some of his favorite dogs. Emmett said that his friend, Andy, was buried so quickly that he "went in the ground warm."

Another story shared by Dennis Williams directly, which came directly from Emmett Forrest, involved Griffith's love of animals, especially dogs. Griffith would go to the pound and tell them to give him two or three of their "sickest dogs." He took the animals home and "mended them." Andy always had five or six dogs on his farm in Manteo, and most Christmas card photos included the dogs.

Emmett Forrest once called the North Carolina Democrat Party furious over an Obama commercial that Andy Griffith was included in that had cost Mount Airy some tourists. As mentioned earlier, Griffith was a Democrat, and Forrest was a Republican, but they remained friends regardless of their divergent political views.

Griffith stated he would not be such a stranger when he returned for the highway dedication in 2002. Andy was a stranger, which was probably due to bad health. I am not aware that he came back again except for Emmett Forrest's wife's funeral on Friday, November 19, 2004, and the TV Land statue dedication.

Eleanor Powell of *The Mount Airy News* tells of a visit to Mount Airy by Andy Griffith, "...when his longtime friend, Emmett Forrest, lost his wife, Barbara King Forrest, from a lengthy illness. He and Cindi came to Mount Airy for the funeral at Grace Moravian Church in 2004. Departing from Mount Airy, the

Griffiths passed by the Andy Griffith Playhouse and paused to look at the Andy Griffith statue erected near the front entrance. With a telephone call to Emmett, Andy jokingly let him know that a bird had laid droppings on his head. Being the friends that they were, Emmett got a bucket of water and washed the bird droppings from Andy's statue."

In 2009, the Andy Griffith Museum opened as a separate building beside the Andy Griffith Playhouse. Owned by the City of Mount Airy, the Surry Arts Council operates the museum. In 2018, the museum underwent renovations that made the exhibits of Smithsonian quality with touchscreen technology, including audio and video, to enhance the experience for the multitude of tourists who visit Andy's hometown each year.

In 2012, as previously stated, I dealt with prostate cancer, with thoughts of mortality, the physical condition it causes for a man, such as bladder control and erectile dysfunction. All this leads to depression, and I fought that. I needed something to bring me out of the dark and get me writing again. I struggled with history projects that I usually dive into, but then I ran into Emmett Forrest on Main Street one day. He too was fighting illness, bladder cancer, I believe, and he said to me after I inquired about his health that it was "like jumping off a ten-story building. Someone asks you about the seventh floor of the fall how you are doing." Emmett answered, "Well, so far, the ride has been pretty good." I marveled at his positive attitude, and as I always did, I asked him if he had spoken to "Mr. Griffith" lately. I never called him Andy because I did not know him personally. Emmett told me about their latest conversation. A month or so later, Andy Griffith died.

When Emmett passed away, Andy's wife, Cindi Griffith, said this of him, "Please understand – Emmett made no money from sharing his collection. It was his gift to the community and to the arts. His entire family… are part of this selfless project. Andy and I understand – along with them, that a town without arts is a sad place to live. Emmett was a true gentleman and an honest man. He was a person I could trust –- a rare thing for Andy and me. He was a loving husband, father, and a very special friend."

After Forrest passed, his daughter gave Lavonda Jessup, who works at Barney's Café and Talley's Custom Frame Shop, the hat Emmett wore. It is on display in the frame shop, where Dennis Williams can see it every day, along with a photo of himself and Emmett from *The Mount Airy News*. After his wife's death, Emmett became reclusive for a while, but eventually came back to society. Forrest told Dennis Williams that he had spent too much time missing her. Williams says now he misses Emmett's stories, especially the ones about growing up in Mount Airy. He says that Forrest was a true "Southern Gentleman."

Emmett said of his friend, Andy, "He left a big footprint." When Emmett passed away in January 2013, he left a big footprint too. This author would say that Emmett and Russell Hiatt are the two people who, along with Andy Griffith, made Mount Airy into Mayberry. Andy Taylor might have said it best. "No matter where life takes you, you always carry in your heart the memories of old times and old friends."

Forrest and Griffith had once pretended Lovill's Creek was the Mississippi River, and they were Tom Sawyer and Huckleberry Finn. Mount Airy owes Forrest and all those who help keep the downtown vibrant a big thank you. All you have to do is visit nearby towns like Stuart or Martinsville in Virginia to see what happens to a small town when the industry leaves, and there is no tourism draw like that of Mount Airy. And to Andy Griffith, the citizens of Mount Airy should say, "I appreciate it."

Emmett Forest shown above with his collection of Andy Griffith items and below with Darrel and Debbie Miles.

Emmett Forrest is shown above left with Mayor Jack Loftis and others opening the Andy Griffith Museum today beside the Surry Arts Council. Emmett, a longtime friend of Andy Griffith, has spent years collecting materials, some from Griffith, which now make up the Andy Griffith Museum collection.

Emmett Forest and his "Bear Bryant" hat are on display at Talley's Custom Frame Shop.

PART FIVE

A VISIT TO MOUNT AIRY

"People started saying that Mayberry was based on Mount Airy...It sure sounds like it, doesn't it...?
I am very happy with the success you've have had with Mayberry. I am proud to be from Mount Airy. I think of you often, and I won't be such a stranger..."
Andy Griffith, October 16, 2002

Things You Might Not Know About Mount Airy

There are Mount Airys in several states such as Maryland, Georgia, Louisiana, Nevada, New Jersey, New York, Ohio, Pennsylvania, and Virginia. From Virginia came the Perkins family, who lived near present day Danville. They named their plantation Mount Airy. The Perkins family were relatives of Civil War General James Ewell Brown "Jeb" Stuart, who grew up outside Mount Airy in Ararat, Patrick County, Virginia.

Known over the years by nicknames such as The Granite City, The Hosiery Capital, The Toaster Capital of the World, The Friendliest City, Small Town USA, and, of course, Mayberry, Mount Airy has a population of just over ten thousand souls in Surry County, which sports over seventy thousand persons. Bordered to the north by Virginia, to the west by Alleghany County, to the east by Stokes County, and Yadkin County to the south, Mount Airy was chartered in 1885.

Drained by the Ararat River and Lovills Creek, which flow through Mount Airy on their way to the Yadkin River. Over the years, the economy thrived first on tobacco until the railroad came in the late ninetieth century, which caused granite from the nearby quarry to ship across the country and the world. Textiles and furniture boomed until the end of the twentieth century, when the loss of jobs to cheaper overseas labor occurred. Today, Mount Airy is boosted by tourism as the mythical Mayberry made famous by native son Andy Griffith.

386

GRANITE

You can see it from outer space, and it gives Mount Airy the nickname Granite City. The world's largest open-faced granite quarry sits in the appropriately named Flat Rock section.

The quarry was operated by the North Carolina Granite Corporation (NCGC) for over 125 years. Their website says that Mount Airy Granite is "the brightest white, most uniform, most available, highest quality, and greatest value granite you will find." Today, the quarry sends granite worldwide, including monuments in Washington, D. C., where it is estimated that 98 percent of the curbing is made of Mount Airy Granite.

The official state rock of North Carolina, Mount Airy Granite, was first used in 1743 but not always appreciated. One story tells of an owner in 1849 who was so enraged finding the "big white rock" on the farm he bought, demanded, and received his money back.

The North Carolina Granite Corporation
PO Box 151, Mount Airy, NC 27030
1.800.227.6242
https://www.ncgranite.com/

Mount Airy was once the "Toaster Capitol of the World."

Toasters To Carports, Textiles To Tourism

The first time I met Jim Grimes at the Mount Airy Chamber of Commerce in the late 1980s to talk about Jeb Stuart and Mount Airy, I will never forget what he said to me. "Mount Airy is the Toaster Capital of the World!" A fact that was confirmed in 1993 when Mount Airy was named the "Toaster Capital of the World."

Proctor Electric Company came to Mount Airy in the late 1950s to build a plant. During construction, they discovered that the plant sat on the grave of Native Peoples that were 300 to 600 years old. The 1.5 million dollar plant became the largest toaster plant in the world.

In 1959, over one million toasters had been manufactured in fifty different models for companies such as Sears, Montgomery Ward, and Universal. They merged in 1960 with the Silex Corporation creating Proctor Silex. Later, the company became Hamilton Beach.

At its height, Mount Airy's plant had 1,000 employees and made thirty-five thousand toasters a day. In the mid-1990s, operations were moved to Mexico after the North American Free Trade Agreement (NAFTA) was signed, ending Mount Airy's reign as the "Toaster Capital."

In my youth, Mount Airy was a boom town with almost zero unemployment. You could walk into any company and get a job. I worked in dye houses in high school, washing socks at Oakdale, and dyeing cloth at Quality Mills after college.

There were multiple industries in the "Granite City," including the North Carolina Granite Corporation. Mount Airy had a vibrant furniture industry that employed people such as Andy Griffith's father, Carl, who operated a band saw at one of the many facilities producing furniture.

The big employer in North Carolina was the textile industry. My grandparents came to the town in the late 1940s to work in textiles as a dynamic duo. My grandmother, Idell Bates Perry, knitted socks, and my grandfather, Erie Perry, fixed the machines she used. In Mount Airy, Spencer's made children's clothes, Quality Mills, later Cross Creek Apparel made mainly golf shirts, Adams Millis, Brown Wooten, Kentucky Derby, Oakdale, and Renfro made all kinds of socks. Today, Nester Hosiery runs the Brown Wooten and Oakdale facilities, and Renfro still manufactures in Mount Airy. Most of the textiles are gone, again due to NAFTA.

Today, Mount Airy has become the "Carport Capital" with over a dozen companies in the area involved in the industry, such as Carolina Carports, Carport Metal Structures, Eagle Carports, HBO Carports, and TNT Carports. Carport Central started in 2014 by brothers Albert and Jay Cara and were named one of the fifty fastest growing companies in Piedmont North Carolina, in 2019.

The industry that keeps Mount Airy's downtown area vibrant is tourism. Andy Griffith is responsible for tourism. Without it, the city would be a ghost town like many of its neighbors, such as Stuart and Martinsville in Virginia, which had similar economies, but no tourism draws such as Mayberry. Today Mount Airy has almost no empty storefronts along Main Street, and tourism related to *The Andy Griffith Show* is responsible for that.

Proctor Electric Company Building Nation's Largest Toaster Plant

Youth Charged With Stealing Gas From Plane

William Otis Ramey, 29, of route 4, Mount Airy, has admitted to police as the person who was seen taking gas from a plane at the Mount Airy Airport Sunday night.

The youth has been charged with trespassing and larceny of gas by L. P. Wrenn, Jr., owner and operator of the airport. Ramey was arrested Monday night and placed under $400 bond.

Three of Ramey's companions were arrested but it is understood they will not be prosecuted as Ramey has confessed to the act and has cleared his friends of any part of the act.

Mr. Wrenn told The NEWS gas has been missing from the planes for some time. He stated that one plane, here from Galax, Va., was left overnight and thieves took some gas from it and failed to replace the cap. It rained later in the night and when the plane took off last Sunday afternoon it had just left the airstrip when the engine failed and the pilot just made it back to the landing strip where a mechanic found water in the tank.

For several days employees of the airport have been staying up and watching for the thieves.

Mr. Wrenn said a car drove up Sunday night about 1:30 o'clock and was taking gas from one of the planes with a water hose. When approached by an airport employee the driver jumped in the car and fled. However, the employee got the license number and recognized the driver.

Mr. Wrenn has issued a plea for young men to leave the planes alone at all times as some prank may result in the death of a pilot.

Mrs. Turnmyre's

PROCTOR PRESIDENT

Walter M. Schwartz, Jr., president of Proctor Electric Company, which is building an ultra-modern toaster factory in Mount Airy. Mr. Schwartz reveals the new factory will be the largest and most modern in America devoted exclusively to the manufacturing of electrical automatic toasters. Other Proctor Products are produced at plants located in Arbutus, Md., and Puerto Rico. Executive offices are in Philadelphia, Pa.

Proctor Electric Company, one of America's foremost housewares manufacturers, is coming to Mount Airy.

Official announcement that Proctor is constructing a plant here on the former Isabel Smith Keary property, was made today by Walter M. Schwartz, Jr., president of the company.

Mr. Schwartz revealed that the ultra-modern plant being constructed here will be devoted exclusively to the manufacturing of electric automatic toasters. Proctor is a pioneer of the industry in this field and the new factory will provide facilities for a considerable increase in production.

In addition to toasters, the company manufactures Mary Proctor Hi-Lo Backsaver Ironing Tables, Sedation Ironing Covers and Pads, both steam and dry irons, Cordminders and Utility Carts.

At the present time, toasters are made in Philadelphia, Pennsylvania, which is also the location of Proctor's executive offices. Irons are produced at a Puerto Rico plant, all other products are manufactured in Baltimore, Maryland. When the Mount Airy plant is completed, the entire toaster operation will be moved here from Philadelphia. However, the executive offices will remain in that city.

Proctor electrical appliances and housewares have long enjoyed successful acceptance with consumers. They are sold in all leading stores from coast-to-coast and advertised extensively on television and in newspapers throughout major market areas.

All Proctor products are officially endorsed and used exclusively by "Mrs. America". The annual "Mrs. America" contest is taking place this week in Fort Lauderdale, Florida.

The company has several outstanding "firsts" in the appliance

392

Things To See In Mount Airy

MOUNT AIRY MUSEUM OF REGIONAL HISTORY

Many do not realize that Mount Airy has a Smithsonian quality history museum. The Mount Airy Museum of Regional History started in 1993 to "Collect, Preserve and Interpret the Natural, Historic, and Artistic Heritage of the Region."
Four floors of the old Merritt Hardware Company on North Main Street tell the story of the area surrounding Surry County, beginning with the natural history and Native Peoples. You will see exhibits permanent, traveling, and visiting, including everything from Mount Airy's old firetrucks in the basement to Donna Fargo and Andy Griffith on the second floor. The third floor will take you through the medical, tobacco, textile, and moonshine. A children's gallery with "Hands on History" is also on the third floor. The top of the clock tower observation room gives visitors a panoramic view of the surrounding area.

Ghost Tours of the downtown area around the museum are available. The museum sponsors a junior historian's program for children in fourth through eighth grades.

The museum is open Tuesday through Saturday and more hours during the warmer months. Admission fees are $6 per person, less for children and seniors.

Mount Airy Museum of Regional History
301 North Main Street, Mount Airy, North Carolina, 27030
Telephone: 336.786.4478
Fax: 336.786.1666
Email:mamrh@northcarolinamuseum.org
www.northcarolinamuseum.org

The Mount Airy Museum of Regional History has an exhibit about the "Granite City's" favorite son, Andy Griffith.

Things To Eat And Drink

SONKER

There is nothing more American than apple pie, and Mount Airy and Surry County are home to the "Sonker," which is a soupy baked dessert or deep-dish pie that is baked nowhere else in the good ole U.S. of A. The Surry County Tourism Partnership has developed a Sonker Trail across the county to give visitors multiple places to taste the fruit-based dessert.

You can find Sonker all over Surry County from Elkin to Pilot Mountain to Dobson and at the Rockford General Store down on the Yadkin River.

Sonker is a deep-dish dessert made of potatoes or fruit, such as pears, blackberries, peaches, or apples. Many people pour a dip over the Sonker as it is served, such as cream, sugar, or molasses. Either way, you make it, Sonker is very yum.

The Pilot Mountain News reported recently about the origin of sonker writing, "The late Cratis Williams, a professor at Appalachian State University, studied and documented Appalachian culture and language. In a Sonker recipe booklet, he suggested that the word 'Sonker' comes from a Scottish word for grassy knoll. I suspect that the appearance of the irregularly shaped piece of dough used in the pie suggested a grass saddle to some imaginative cook, and the name of the pie came into being,' wrote Williams about Sonker."

The Surry County Historical Society has hosted a Sonker Festival on the first Saturday of October every year for thirty-five years at the Edwards-Franklin House on Haystack Road west of Mount Airy off Highway 89 beyond Interstate 77.

http://sonkertrail.org

World Famous Pork Chop Sandwich

Charles Dowell started working at the Snappy Lunch in 1943, sweeping and cleaning. Seventeen years later, he was the owner and began to develop his recipes, including the very messy and very tasty "World Famous Pork Chop Sandwich." The sandwich includes a pork chop, coleslaw, mustard, and chili.

This is the only business still in operation mentioned on *The Andy Griffith Show* in "Andy The Matchmaker" episode. Andy suggests to Barney that they get a bite to eat at the Snappy Lunch.

Andy was known for his love of hot dogs that he carried on to *Matlock*, but it was here at the Snappy Lunch that he got a hot dog and a bottle of pop in real life. Charles Dowell once said, "We serve white bread when we opened, and we serve white bread now. Why mess with anything else? Keeping it simple is part of the secret, and simple is what I grew up with."

The Ground Steak Sandwich Recipe

2 lbs. ground chuck (80/20 is crucial to the success)
    1/4 cup flour
    3/4 cup water
    1/2 teaspoon salt
    pepper

1. Start by browning the beef in the pan, chopping up, so the meat takes on a "sloppy joe" appearance.
2. Drain ground meat.
3. Pepper meat LIBERALLY! This is supposed to be redolent in the taste of ground black pepper.
4. Whisk together water, salt, and flour.
5. Add to skillet, and allow to come to a boil.
6. Lower heat and simmer until the mixture has thickened.
7. Serve on buns with mayo, your favorite coleslaw, and a slice of tomato.

Ground Steak Sandwich

"Boil the meat, drain the grease, and add salt, pepper, flour, and water." Mount Airy has a sandwich no one else has, the ground steak. It was believed to have started during the Great Depression to make beef last.

Where to eat one in Mount Airy:

The Dairy Center

407 West Lebanon Street

The Speedy Chef

1516 South Main Street

The Snappy Lunch

125 North Main Street

Odell's Sandwich Shop

1224 West Pine Street

Aunt Bea's

452 N Andy Griffith Pkwy

Flat Rock Ruritans

Sells them at the Autumn Leaves Festival.

The Loaded Goat

Jimmy, The Loaded Goat, comes from The Andy Griffith Show episode in Season 3, Episode 18. It is a great place for a gourmet burger or Betty Lynn's birthday every year.

247 City Hall St. Mount Airy, North Carolina, 27030
Phone: 336-755-3627
Email: loadedgoatowner@gmail.com
www.theloadedgoat.com

Walker's Soda Fountain

Doug Jones is a real "Soda Jerk" and a nice guy. His family operates Walker's in the old Lamm's Drug Store. Open every day except Tuesday.

175 N Main St, Mt Airy, NC 27030
336-786-4006
mayberrysodafountain@live.com
https://www.visitnc.com/listing/BsLM/walker-s-soda-fountain

Mayberry Spirits

One of Mount Airy's newest and innovative businesses gives a great tour about how they put the spirit into Mayberry.

461 N South Street, Mount Airy, North Carolina
336-719-6860
http://www.mayberryspirits.com/

Barney's Cafe

A great place to eat breakfast or lunch on Main Street with Security By Fife is open every day except Sunday.

206 N Main St, Mt Airy, North Carolina 27030

336-786-8305

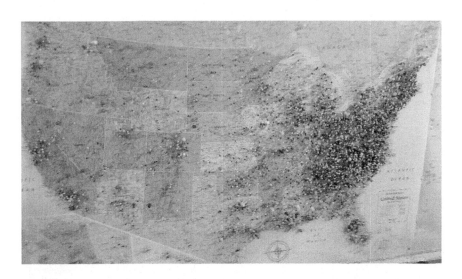

**Barney's Café has maps with push pins from all over the USA
and the World of people who have visited Mount Airy looking
for Mayberry.**

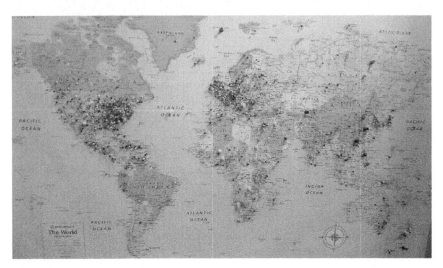

Breakfast with the Bradshaws and Ted Womack at Barney's.

Leon's

Celebrating thirty years on Main Street is a great place for breakfast or lunch. Be sure to try their famous California Burger.

407 N Main Street, Mount Airy, North Carolina 27030

336-789-0849

Market and Franklin Streets

Everything from craft beer, yoga, video games, and many restaurants is part of the newly developed areas along Market and Franklin Streets, a block south of Main Street in Mount Airy.

You never know who you might meet in Mayberry.

TROY
NORTH CAROLINA

WIFE OF THE SHERIFF OF MAYBERRY

Barbara Bray Edwards married Andy Griffith, actor and star of the Andy Griffith Show, in 1949. Her father was the school superintendent of Montgomery County schools. The Edwards' home was near here. She and Griffith returned to Troy often to visit her family. She died in 1980 and is buried in Los Angeles, Ca.

Andy's first wife, Barbara, was recently honored in her hometown of Troy, North Carolina.

They Came From Mount Airy

ANNA WOOD

Mount Airy has a long history of entertainers who called the Granite City home, including the Siamese Twins, Eng and Chang Bunker, and, of course, Andy Griffith. A new generation continues the trend. Before going to the North Carolina School of the Arts in nearby Winston-Salem, North Carolina, Anna Wood attended Mount Airy public schools.

After graduation, she starred in several television programs, including a very blue woman in USA networks *Royal Pains*. Other appearances include those in Showtime's *House of Lies* and AMC's memorable *Mad Men*. Wood appeared in six episodes of NBC's prime=time soap opera *Deception* and as Jamie Sawyers in the CBS's legal drama *Reckless,* set in Charleston, South Carolina. Anna starred in *The Code* on CBS in 2019.

Anna's movie roles include *The Layla Project, Nice Guy Johnny, Negative Space,* and *Chronicle.* The latter's cast included Dane DeHaan, famous for his role as the Green Goblin in *The Amazing Spider Man 2*, whom Wood married on June 30, 2012. The couple started dating while at the North Carolina School of the Arts. They reside in Brooklyn, New York.

COACH FRANK BEAMER

Coach Frank Beamer was born in the Martin Hospital on Cherry Street in Mount Airy in October 1946. When he retired in 2015, he was the winningest active coach in college football. While more associated with Fancy Gap, Carroll County, Virginia, where he grew up, the Virginia Tech Head Football Coach had 280 wins (238 at Virginia Tech),

After playing at Hillsville High School, Beamer played in the defensive backfield at Virginia Tech from 1966-69, playing in two Liberty Bowls. He led Virginia Tech to twenty-three straight bowl games, the longest active streak during his career 1987-2015.

Beamer's teams are known for playing Beamerball, which means that the defense and special teams score along with the offense. Beamer coached special teams himself and was known for blocking the opposing team's kicks, leading to Virginia Tech's points.

In 1999, Virginia Tech went undefeated, led by quarterback Michael Vick's stellar play, and earned a spot in the National Championship Game against Florida State. He coached his teams to eight conference championships. In 2018, the College Football Hall of Fame inducted Beamer as a member.

SIAMESE TWINS

The subject of several books and stories by Mark Twain, The World Famous Siamese Twins, Eng and Chang Bunker, called Mount Airy home for the later stages of their incredible life. They rest today, joined together in death as they were in life, near their homes on Stewart's Creek.

Born in 1811 in Siam, today known as Thailand, in Southeast Asia, the boys were lucky to survive in a time when their birth was seen as an evil foreboding. Discovered by a ship captain, the conjoined twins made their way to Europe and America, where they spent decades performing.

They came to North Carolina, first to Wilkes County, southwest of Surry County, where they met and married sisters. The four had over twenty children. Two sons even served in the Confederate cavalry during the War Between the States.

Each year over 1,000 descendants of the Bunker Twins come to Mount Airy for a family reunion. Chang and Eng were conjoined at the abdomen via cartilage and shared a liver and a belly button, both of which they only had one, but in all other ways, they were two separate beings.

Separated after their deaths in 1874, the brothers were kept for a time in the basement of one of their houses due to fears of grave robbers. The Bunkers were eventually buried at the nearby White Plains Baptist Church with their wives.

J. E. B. STUART

James Ewell Brown "Jeb" Stuart was born just outside Mount Airy in Ararat, Patrick County, Virginia, on February 6, 1833. The Stuarts attended church in Mount Airy with the congregation that later became Trinity Episcopal Church. They shopped and picked up their mail in town, where Stuart often wrote that people should "Write to me at Mount Airy, North Carolina." James Stuart graduated from West Point in 1854 and served for seven years in the United States Army in the Kansas Territory. In 1861, Stuart resigned and returned to Virginia, where he found himself a colonel in the 1st Virginia Cavalry. He fought at the First Battle of Manassas and received a promotion to brigadier general. In 1862, Stuart rode around the Union Army three times, serving as commander of Robert E. Lee's Army of Northern Virginia's cavalry. He received a promotion to major general. In 1863, Stuart took the place of the wounded Thomas J. "Stonewall" Jackson, commanding an entire infantry corps at the Battle of Chancellorsville. In June, Stuart led the Confederate Cavalry of ten thousand at one of the largest cavalry fights ever in the Western Hemisphere at the Battle of Brandy Station. A month later, Stuart's absence on the first day of Gettysburg's Battle led to a controversy. Stuart lost his life the day after receiving a wound at the hands of one of George Custer's men at the Battle of Yellow Tavern, just north of Richmond, Virginia. J. E. B. Stuart died on May 12, 1864, and is buried at Hollywood Cemetery in Richmond.

DONNA FARGO

The "Happiest Girl In The Whole USA" called Mount Airy home. Born Yvonne Vaughn, the country singer went west to California after graduating from High Point College.

In 1969, the Academy of Country Music named Donna Fargo the Best New Female Vocalist. In 1972, she had two number one country singles with "The Happiest Girl In The Whole USA" and "Funny Face." Both singles crossed over to the pop charts. The former was named Best Single, Best Song, and Best Album in 1972 by the Academy of Country Music and Single of the Year by the Country Music Association.

In 1978, Fargo had a television show. That same year she was diagnosed with multiple sclerosis. She continued to record up through 1991. Since then, she has authored books and developed a line of greeting cards.

An exhibit about her life is on permanent display at the Mount Airy Museum of Regional History. She often returns to Mount Airy. In 2012, she was July Fourth Parade Grand Marshall. Part of Highway 103, East Pine Street, was named the Donna Fargo Highway as it goes by her former home near the Blue Hollow section of Surry County.

MAYBERRY MOTOR INN AND THE AUNT BEE ROOM

Before she owned the Mayberry Motor Inn, Alma Venable fixed Andy Griffith's mother Geneva's hair. Today, her motel is famous for the Aunt Bee Room dedicated to The Andy Griffith Show's character.

Alma started her Aunt Bee Room on June 1, 1990, when she attended an auction of Francis Bavier's estate. The first piece of furniture she bought was a vanity. Today, the room holds a twin bedroom suite and certificates of authenticity for more than thirty items that belonged to Bavier, such as gloves, eyeglasses, a handkerchief, a dress, a hat, a shoe kit, an attaché case, and sewing materials.

Alma dresses up as an Aunt Bee tribute artist during the annual Mayberry Days celebration in Mount Airy. Alma likes visitors to enjoy a window's view of the Aunt Bee Room, but Alma might let you have an even closer look at Aunt Bee's stuff if she is there.

While staying at the twenty-seven room motel, you can see a Mayberry Squad Car, Emmett's pickup truck, a gazebo. Guests can walk along Thelma Lou's trail and enjoy the flowers and pool when in season.

501 Andy Griffith Parkway North
Phone: (336) 786-4109,
Email: mayberry@surry.net
Fax 336-789-9819
www.mayberrymotorinn.com

424

ANDY GRIFFITH'S HOMEPLACE

While visiting Mount Airy, you can stay in the house where Andy Griffith grew up and was his parent's home until 1966. It is not his birthplace as he was born a few blocks away on South Street. Today, the house can be accessed through the Hampton Inn on Highway 601, about a mile away.

Andy's room is in the back of the house, just off the kitchen. Often you will see people ride by on a Squad Car Tour. The house is just across the street and under the giant water tower that holds Andy and Opie's image headed for the fishing hole at Myers Lake.

Andy's Homeplace

711 E. Haymore Street

Phone: (336) 789-5999

Email: Lenise.Lynch@hilton.com

https://www.visitnc.com/listing/andy-s-homeplace

MAYBERRY CAMPGROUND

If you have an RV and want to stay on historic ground, the Mayberry Campground is the place for you. Built on land that once belonged to Eng and Chang Bunker, the Siamese Twins, who married two North Carolina sisters from nearby Wilkes County, and then moved to Surry County, where they raised twenty-one children between the four parents.

The house of William Bunker, son of Eng Bunker, is available for tours and is the property's centerpiece. There are over one hundred RV sites, including back in and pull through sites available.

The campground is located just off Interstate 74 and Highway 601, giving the park easy access to travelers and reaching a Walmart and a Cracker Barrel.

114 Bunker Road

Phone: (336) 789-6199

http://www.mayberrycampground.com/

WOLF CREEK FARM

     This B&B located in the Blue Ridge Mountains foothills, Wolf Creek Farm, is a marvelous private place just to put your feet up and relax. Fish in our 5-acre lake, hike the trails, swim in our in-ground private pool, or do nothing! Visit Mt. Airy, NC ("Mayberry"), do a wine-tasting at one of our nearby wineries or enjoy breath-taking vistas on the Blue Ridge Parkway just minutes away. Our mile-long paved drive is motorcycle-friendly. We have special in-door parking for our motorcycle enthusiasts!

http://www.wolfcreekfarmva.net/

Phone: (800) 416-9653

Email: wolfcreekmimi@gmail.com

Places To Shop in Mount Airy

Mount Airy is different from many small southern towns that lose their downtown shopping areas to malls. In Mount Airy, the downtown is thriving, and here are some of the recommended shops. I encourage you to visit Andy Griffith's hometown during your visit and get one of my other books.

Mayberry Markets & Souvenirs

Another place to find all things Mayberry and where you will find this author during Mayberry Days Parade on Saturday.

182 North Main Street
336-719-2363
mayberrymarket@gmail.com
https://mayberrymarkets.com

Opie's Candy Shop

135 North Main Street
Phone: 336-786-1960
Email: info@opiescandystore.com
https://www.opiescandystore.com/

Located beside Floyd's City Barbershop, this the place to get your sweet tooth while visiting Main Street.

Bear Creek Gifts and Fudge Factory

Jerry Caudle was one of the original Mayberry merchants on Main Street. He operates a wonderful place to get fudge and all things Mayberry.

165 N Main Street Mount Airy North Carolina 27030
Phone: 336-786-6602
mayberrycandles@hotmail.com
www.bearcreekfudge.com

Miss Angels Heavenly Pies

The smell emanating from this store is heavenly, and the desserts are excellent.

153 North Main Street
Mount Airy, NC 27030
Phone: 336-786-1537
Email: info@missangelsheavenlypiesinc.com
https://www.missangelsheavenlypiesinc.com/

Talley's Custom Frame And Gallery

I started selling books all those years ago, and it is a suitable place to frame something from Mayberry. You will find me in front of this store during the Autumn Leaves Festival every October.

212 N Main Street

(336)-786-4696

talleygallery@embarqmail.com

Mayberry Country

Another place to find all things Mayberry, get a pizza next door while enjoying the big Coca-Cola ghost image in Canteen Alley next door and get one of my books from the rack.

187 N Main Street

(336)-786-4488

Mayberry On Main

Operated by Esther Cortez and her husband, Scott Freeman, and daughter, Ashton, shown here with Betty Lynn. They own and operate The Loaded Goat too.

192 North Main Street

mayberryonmain@gmail.com

Mayberry Antique Mall

One of my favorite places on Main Street in Mount Airy has two racks of my books available.

160 North Main St.

(336)-755-2023

mayberryantiquemall@yahoo.com

http://www.mayberryantiquemall.com/

Mill Creek General Store

A beautiful place for healthy food with two racks of my books is located across from Andy Griffith's birthplace at the corner of Pine and South Streets.

541 West Pine Street, Suite 200

Phone: (336)-755-2340

https://www.millcreekgeneralstore.com

The Corn Crib

The Corn Crib will be your one stop shop for antiques, primitives, farmhouses, candles, handmade crafts, and much more!!!

2638 Riverside Drive, Mount Airy, North Carolina

Phone: (336) 719-0499

Gold Leaf Treasures

Carroll Byrd will tell tobacco was king in this neck of the woods, Henry County, Virginia. In his store, he still operates with his wife, Margie, and brother-in-law, Donny Clark.

192 N Main Street

Phone: (336) 719-1582

The Mount Airy Museum of Regional History sponsors a Badge Drop on New Year's Eve. Even the local llamas enjoy the spectacle bringing in the new year.

Selected Bibliography

Patrick County Deed Book 30 page 509
Patrick County Marriage Register Volume 5 page 27
Patrick County Land Book 1925
Patrick County Historical Society
      Nunn Family File

Books

Claiborne, Jack, and Price, William, editors. *Discovering North Carolina: A Tar Heel Reader.*

Collins, Terry. *Andy Griffith: An Illustrated Biography*, Mount Airy, 1995.

Smith, O. Norris. *The Nunns of 18th Century Virginia*. Greensboro NC.

Articles

American Profile: October 1, 2005.

Readers Digest
      "He Never Left Home"

Our State: Down Home in North Carolina.
      October 2005, Volume 71, Number 5
      Andy Says "Hey" page 32
      Festival of Color page 116
      Mayberry Bound page 120
      July 2012, Volume 80, Number 2
      Mayberry page 86

Wachovia Moravian, February 1968, Vol.78 No.2
      "The Andy Griffith I Knew" by Edward T. Mickey, Jr.

Newspapers

Brunswick News, December 13, 2019
Cleveland This Week April 16, 1967
Denver Post July 6, 2012, "Andy Griffith's Denver Based Daughter"
The Enterprise April 23, 2005, article by Fred Gilley
Mount Airy News
"Griffiths Say Goodbye To Friendly City Today," April 1966
"Andy Griffith Praised As Only Man To Ever Add Whole Town NC—Mayberry," October 13, 1978
"Music Was One Of Griffith's First Loves," March 29, 1992

"Andy says it was a thrill visiting his boyhood home," March 27, 2003
"Churches using Andy Griffith Show…," December 18, 2005
"Two cancel travel plans due to ad by Andy Griffith," June 2010
"Andy Griffith rebuilds ties with church," July 2009
"Lessons Andy Griffith could teach to all of us by," July 2012
"Andy Griffith left imprint on 'Mayberry' residents," July 4, 2012
"Andy's relationship with hometown was tragic," July 5, 2012
"Otis Files Lawsuit Against Police, City," July 12, 2012
Other dates: June 26, 1993; October 23, 2002; September 24, 2004; September 19, 2019.

Mount Airy Times
"Andy Griffith Given Going Away Party," July 21, 1944
"City Plans Huge Andy Day," May 31, 1957
Other dates: July 15, 1947; January 28, 1949; September 16, 1949; July 30, 1961.

Topeka Capital Journal,
"Topekan from 'Mayberry' celebrates Griffith," July 3, 2012

Winston-Salem Journal
"After Setbacks, Griffith Finds Deep Happiness," November 10, 1984
"Andy Is Mighty Proud To Return To Mayberry," April 12, 1986
"Memory: Cousin Recalls Andy Griffith's Boyhood," September 1990
"The Pride of Mount Airy," July 4, 2012

The Wachovia Moravian
"The Andy Griffith I Know." February 1968

<u>Video</u>
Andy Griffith: Hollywood's Homespun Hero, 1997.
North Carolina People with William Friday, December 1993.

<u>Interviews</u>
Darrel and Debbie Miles
Dennis Williams

Acknowledgments

Special thanks to Ace Snyder and Jack Riekehof-Snyder.

Thanks to Charles A. Brintle, Patricia and Benjamin Comire, Charles and Mary Agnes Dowell, Emmett Forrest, Jennifer Gregory, Debbie Hall, Russell Hiatt, R. Wayne Jones, and Darrel and Debbie Miles. Special thanks to Amy E. Snyder for getting me started and seeing me through my illness twice.

Photo Credits
Photos courtesy of the Surry County Historical Society Minick Collection, Mount Airy Museum of Regional History, Mayberry on Main, R. Wayne Jones, Mount Airy News, Winston-Salem Journal, Denver Post, Virginia Pilot, Darrel and Debbie Miles, Samantha Hanneman, Allen and Judy Burton, Donna Davidson Rogers, Dennis Williams, Lavonda Jessup, Ted Womack, and the author's collection.

Mayberry Trading Post along the Blue Ridge Parkway.

Related Websites

Mount Airy Visitors Center www.visitmayberry.com

Surry Arts Council http://www.surryarts.org

Mount Airy Museum of Regional History
www.northcarolinamuseum.org

Surry County Tourism www.verysurry.com

Squad Car Tours www.tourmayberry.com

Snappy Lunch www.thesnappylunch.com

Mayberry on Main
www.facebook.com/notifications#!/mayberryonmain

North Carolina Granite Corporation www.ncgranite.com

Talley's Custom Frame Shop www.facebook.com/pages/Talleys-Custom-Frame-Gallery/185955838100107

Miss Angels https://www.missangelsheavenlypiesinc.com/

Bear Creek Fudge www.bearcreekfudge.com

Mayberry Market and Souvenirs https://mayberrymarkets.com

Opie's Candy Store https://www.opiescandystore.com/

Mayberry Campground www.mayberrymotorinn.com

Mayberry Spirits http://www.mayberryspirits.com/

Walker's Soda Fountain
https://www.visitnc.com/listing/BsLM/walker-s-soda-fountain

The Loaded Goat www.theloadedgoat.com

The Snappy Lunch http://www.thesnappylunch.com/

Sonker Trail http://sonkertrail.org

Mayberry Antique Mall http://www.mayberryantiquemall.com/

Historian Tom Perry at the site he saved, J. E. B. Stuart's Birthplace, the Laurel Hill Farm, just outside Mount Airy in Patrick County, Virginia.

About The Author

J. E. B. Stuart's biographer, Emory Thomas, describes Tom Perry as "a fine and generous gentleman who grew up near Laurel Hill, where Stuart grew up, has founded J. E. B. Stuart Birthplace, and attracted considerable interest in the preservation of Laurel Hill. He has started a symposium series about aspects of Stuart's life to sustain interest in Stuart beyond Ararat, Virginia." Perry graduated from Patrick County High School in 1979 and Virginia Tech in 1983 with a bachelor's degree in history.

Tom founded the J. E. B. Stuart Birthplace in 1990. The non-profit organization has preserved 75 acres of the Stuart property, including the house site where J. E. B. Stuart was born on February 6, 1833. Perry wrote the eight interpretive signs about Laurel Hill's history along with the Virginia Civil War Trails sign and the new Virginia Historical Highway Marker in 2002. He spent many years researching and traveling all over the nation to find Stuart materials. He continues his work to preserve Stuart's Birthplace, producing the Laurel Hill Teacher's Guide for educators and the Laurel Hill Reference Guide for groups.

Perry can be seen on Virginia Public Television's *Forgotten Battlefields: The Civil War in Southwest Virginia*, with his mentor, noted Civil War Historian Dr. James I. Robertson, Jr. Perry has begun a collection of papers relating to Stuart and Patrick County's history in the Special Collections Department of the Carol M. Newman Library at Virginia Tech under the auspices of the Virginia Center for Civil War Studies.

Historian Thomas D. Perry is the author and publisher of over forty books on regional history in Virginia surrounding his home county of Patrick. He is the author of ten books on Patrick County, Virginia, including *Ascent to Glory, The Genealogy of J. E.*

B. Stuart, *The Free State of Patrick: Patrick County Virginia in the Civil War, The Dear Old Hills of Patrick: J. E. B. Stuart and Patrick County, Virginia, Images of America: Patrick County Virginia,* and *Notes From The Free State Of Patrick.*

For a decade, Perry taught Civil War history to every eleventh-grade history class at his alma mater, Patrick County High School, from his book *The Free State of Patrick: Patrick County Virginia in the Civil War.* He can be seen in Henrico County, Virginia's DVD documentary *Bold Dragoon: The Life of J. E. B. Stuart.*

http://henrico-va.granicus.com/MediaPlayer.php?clip_id=1088

Perry was a featured presenter at the Virginia Festival of the Book in 2012. He speaks all over the country on topics as far ranging as Andy Griffith to J. E. B. Stuart.

In 2004, Perry began The Free State of Patrick Internet History Group, which became the largest historical organization in the area, with over 500 members. It covered Patrick County, Virginia, and regional history. Tom produced a monthly email newsletter about regional history entitled *Notes From The Free State of Patrick.*

In 2009, Perry used his book Images of America Henry County, Virginia, to raise over $25,000 for the Bassett Historical Center, "The Best Little Library in Virginia," and as editor of the Henry County Heritage Book raised another $30,000. Perry was responsible for over $200,000 of the $800,000 raised to expand the regional history library.

He is the recipient of the John E. Divine Award from the Civil War Education Association, the Hester Jackson Award from the Surry County Civil War Round Table, and the Best Article Award from the Society of North Carolina Historians for his article on Stoneman's Raid in 2008. In 2010, he received an acknowledgment from the Bassett Public Library Association for his work to expand the Bassett Historical Center and was named Henry County, Virginia Man of the Year by www.myhenrycounty.com. The Sons of the American Revolution presented Tom with the Good Citizenship Award. Perry also recently received the National Society of the Daughters of the American Revolution Community Service Award from the Patrick Henry Daughters of the American Revolution.

Perry has remembered the history of those who helped him. He worked with the Virginia Department of Transportation to name the bridge over the Dan River after his neighbor, Command Sergeant Major Zeb Stuart Scales, who was the most decorated non-commissioned soldier from Patrick County, Virginia. Perry remembered his teachers at Blue Ridge Elementary School, including his father, Erie Perry, who was a teacher and principal for thirty years in The Free State of Patrick, by placing a monument to the retired teachers at the school in Ararat, Virginia.

Perry, a recognized authority on J. E. B. Stuart, is presently working on a three-volume projected titled The Papers of J. E. B. Stuart.

Mount Airy
North Carolina

HISTORY AND MEMORY SERIES
FROM LAUREL HILL PUBLISHING

THOMAS D. PERRY

Also Available From Tom Perry's Laurel Hill Publishing

MAYBERRY TRIVIA

1,500 QUESTIONS ABOUT A TV CLASSIC

SCOTT HOPKINS

Also available from Tom Perry's Laurel Hill Publishing

Andy Griffith barefoot in Mount Airy

Made in the USA
Monee, IL
22 October 2021